Withdrawn

GEOS
the prentice hall custom laboratory program for the earth sciences

Geography 102OL

Physical Environment Laboratory

Director of Database Publishing: Michael Payne
Executive Marketing Manager: Nathan L. Wilbur
Operations Manager: Eric M. Kenney
Assistant Editor: Emily A. Colangelo
Development Editor: Amy Galvin
Production Project Manager: Jennifer Berry
Database Project Specialist: Zach LaRosa
Cover Designer: Renee Sartell

Cover Art: Courtesy of Photolibrary.com, Robert Harding World Imagery, Getty Images/Photodisc.

This special edition published in cooperation with Pearson Custom Publishing.

Printed in the United States of America.

Please visit our web site at *www.pearsoncustom.com*

Attention bookstores: For permission to return unused stock, call 800-777-6872.

ISBN-13: 978-0-558-03934-9
ISBN-10: 0-558-03934-0

Package ISBN-13: N/A
Package ISBN-10: N/A

PEARSON CUSTOM PUBLISHING
501 Boylston Street, Suite 900
Boston, MA 02116

CONTENTS

The Metric System, Measurements, and Scientific Inquiry

Earth science, the study of Earth and its neighbors in space, involves investigations of natural objects that range in size from the very smallest divisions of atoms to the largest of galaxies (Figure 1). From atoms to galaxies, objects are each unique in their size, mass, and volume; and yet all are related when it comes to understanding the nature of Earth and its place in the universe.

Almost every scientific investigation requires accurate measurements. One important purpose of this exercise is to examine the metric system as a method of scientific measurement used in the Earth sciences. In addition, a few special units of measurement are also examined. The exercise concludes with an activity that focuses on the nature of scientific inquiry.

Objectives

After you have completed this exercise, you should be able to:

1. List the units for length, mass, and volume that are used in the metric system.
2. Use the metric system for measurements.
3. Convert units within the metric system.
4. Understand and use the micrometer and nanometer for measuring very small distances as well as the astronomical unit and light-year for measuring large distances.
5. Determine the approximate density and specific gravity of a solid substance.
6. Conduct a scientific experiment using accepted methods of scientific inquiry.

Materials

metric ruler   calculator

Materials Supplied by Your Instructor

metric tape measure or meterstick	paper clip	nickel coin
	paper cup	small rock
metric balance	thread	
"bathroom" scale (metric)	large graduated cylinder (marked in milliliters)	

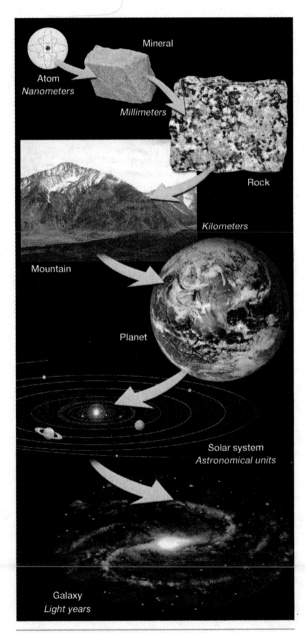

Figure 1 The range of Earth science measurements.

Terms

metric system	micrometer	light-year
meter	(or micron)	density
liter	nanometer	specific gravity
gram	astronomical unit	hypothesis
Celsius degrees	Kelvin degrees	

Introduction

To describe objects, Earth scientists use units of measurement that are relative to the particular feature being studied. For example, centimeters or inches, instead of kilometers or miles, would be used to measure the width of this page; and kilometers or miles, rather than centimeters or inches, to measure the distance from New York to London, England.

Most areas of science have developed units of measurement that meet their particular needs. However, regardless of the unit used, all scientific measurements are defined within a broader system so that they may be understood and compared. In science, the fundamental units have been established by the *International System of Units* (SI, Système International d'Unités) (Table 1).

The Metric System

The **metric system** is a decimal system (based on fractions or multiples of ten) that uses only one basic unit for each type of measurement: the **meter** (m) as the

unit of length (Figure 2), the **liter** (l) as the unit of volume (One liter is equal to the volume of one kilogram of pure water at 4°C (39.2°F), about 1.06 quarts.), and the **gram** (g) as the unit of mass (Figure 3). In the English system, the units used to express the same relations are feet, quarts, and ounces.

METER (m)

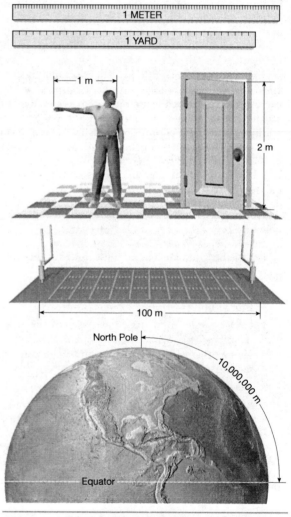

Figure 2 The SI unit of length is the meter (m), which is slightly longer than a yard. Originally described as one ten-millionth of the distance from the equator to the North Pole, it is currently defined as the distance traveled by light in a vacuum in 0.0000000033 of a second.

Table 1 Base units of the SI. From these base units, other units are derived to express quantities such as power (watt, W), force (newton, N), energy (joule, J), and pressure (pascal, Pa).

Unit	Quantity measured	Symbol
meter	length	m
kilogram	mass	kg
second	time	s
kelvin	thermodynamic temperature	K
ampere	electric current	A
mole	quantity of a substance	mol
candela	luminous intensity	cd

GRAM (g)

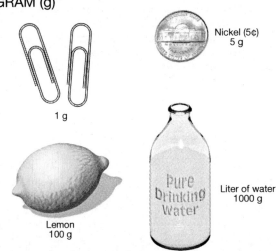

Figure 3 The basic unit of mass in the metric system is the gram (g), approximately equal to the mass of one cubic centimeter of pure water at 4°C (39.2°F). A gram is about the weight of two paper clips, while an ounce is about the weight of 40 paper clips.

Working with the Metric System

In the metric system the basic units of weights and measures are in "tens" relations to each other. It is similar to our monetary system where 10 pennies equal one dime and 10 dimes equal one dollar. However, in the English system of weights and measures no such regularity exists; for example, 12 inches equal a foot and 5,280 feet equal a statute mile. Thus, the advantage of the metric system is *consistency.*

Table 2 illustrates the prefixes that are used in the metric system to indicate how many times more (in multiples of 10) or what fraction (in fractions of ten) of the basic unit you have. Therefore, from the information in the table, a *kilo*gram (kg) means one thousand grams, while a *milli*gram (mg) is one one-thousandth of a gram.

To familiarize yourself with metric units, determine the following measurements using the equipment provided in the laboratory.

Measuring length:

1. Use a metric measuring tape (or meterstick) to measure your height as accurately as possible to the nearest hundredth of a meter (called a centimeter).

    _____ . _____ meters (m)

2. Use a metric ruler to measure the length of this page as accurately as possible to the nearest tenth of a centimeter (called a millimeter).

    _____ . _____ centimeters (cm)

3. Accurately measure the length of your shoe to the nearest millimeter.

    _____ millimeters (mm)

Measuring volume:

4. Use a graduated measuring cylinder to measure the volume of the paper cup to the nearest milliliter.

    _____ milliliters (ml)

Table 2   Metric Prefixes and Symbols

Prefix[1]	Symbol[2]	Meaning
giga-	G	one billion times base unit (1,000,000,000 × base)
mega-	M	one million times base unit (1,000,000 × base)
kilo-	k	one thousand times base unit (1000 × base)
hecto-	h	one hundred times base unit (100 × base)
deka-	da	ten times base unit (10 × base)
BASE UNIT	m (meter)–base unit of length l (liter)–base unit of volume g (gram)–base unit of mass	
deci-	d	one-tenth times base unit (.1 × base)
centi-	c	one-hundredth times base unit (.01 × base)
milli-	m	one-thousandth times base unit (.001 × base)
micro-	μ	one-millionth times base unit (.000001 × base)
nano-	n	one-billionth times base unit (.000000001 × base)

[1]A prefix is added to the base unit to indicate how many times more, or what fraction of, the base unit is present. For example, a kilometer (km) means one thousand meters and a millimeter (mm) means one thousandth of a meter.
[2]When writing in the SI system, periods are not used after the unit symbols and symbols are not made plural. For example, if the length of a stick is 50 centimeters, it would be written as "50 cm" (not "50 cm." or "50 cms").

Measuring mass:

5. Weigh the following and record your results. (Follow the directions of your instructor for using a metric balance.)

Sample of rock: _____ grams (g)

Paper clip: _____ grams (g)

Nickel coin: _____ grams (g)

(*Note:* Two terms that are often confused are *mass* and *weight*. Mass is a measure of the amount of matter an object contains. Weight is a measure of the force of gravity on an object. For example, the mass of an object would be the same on both Earth and the Moon. However, because the gravitational force of the Moon is less than that of Earth, the object would weigh less on the Moon. On Earth, mass and weight are directly related, and often the same units are used to express each.)

6. Use the metric "bathroom" scale. Weigh yourself as accurately as possible to the nearest tenth of a kilogram. (*Note:* If a metric scale is not available, convert your weight in pounds to kilograms by multiplying your weight (in pounds) by 0.45.)

_____ . _____ kilograms (kg)

Metric Conversions

As stated earlier, one important advantage of the metric system is that it is based on "tens." As shown on the metric conversion diagram, Figure 4, conversion from one unit to another can be accomplished simply by *moving the decimal point* to the left if going to larger units, or by moving the decimal point to the right if going to smaller units.

For example, if you measure the length of a piece of string and it is 1.43 decimeters long, in order to convert its length to millimeters, start with 1.43 on the "deci-" step of the diagram. Then move the decimal two places (steps) to the right (the "milli-" step). The length, in millimeters, becomes 143.0 millimeters.

7. Use the metric conversion diagram, Figure 4, to convert the following:

a. 2.05 meters (m) = _____ centimeters (cm)

b. 1.50 meters (m) = _____ millimeters (mm)

c. 9.81 liters (l) = _____ deciliters (dl)

d. 5.4 grams (g) = _____ milligrams (mg)

e. 6.8 meters (m) = _____ kilometer (km)

f. 4,214.6 centimeters = _____ meters (m)

g. 321.50 grams = _____ kilogram (kg)

h. 70.73 hectoliters = _____ dekaliters (dal)

8. Use a metric tape measure (or meterstick) to determine the length of your laboratory table as accurately as possible to the nearest hundredth of a meter. Then convert the length to each of the units in question 8b.

a. Length of table: _____ . _____ meters

b. Length of table equals:

_____ millimeters (mm)

_____ centimeters (cm)

_____ km

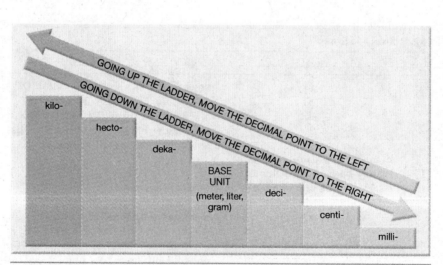

Figure 4   Metric conversion diagram. Beginning at the appropriate step, if going to larger units (left), move the decimal to the left for each step crossed. When going to smaller units (right), move the decimal to the right for each step crossed. For example, 1.253 meters (base unit step) would be equivalent to 1,253.0 millimeters (decimal moved three steps to the right, the milli- step).

Metric–English Conversions

Because the change to the metric system will occur gradually over the next few decades, we will be forced to use both systems simultaneously. If we are not able to convert from one system to the other, we will occasionally be inconvenienced or mildly frustrated.

By using the conversion tables on the inside back cover of this manual, show the metric equivalent for each of the following units.

Length conversion:

9. 1 inch = _____ centimeters

10. 1 meter = _____ feet

11. 1 mile = _____ kilometers

Volume conversion:

12. 1 gallon = _____ liters

13. 1 cubic centimeter = _____ cubic inch

Mass conversion:

14. 1 gram = _____ ounce

15. 1 pound = _____ kilogram

Temperature

Temperature represents one relatively common example of using different systems of measurement. On the Fahrenheit temperature scale, 32°F is the melting point of ice and 212°F marks the boiling point of water (at standard atmospheric pressure). On the **Celsius scale**, ice melts at 0°C and water boils at 100°C. On the **Kelvin scale**, ice melts at 273 K.

Conversion from one temperature scale to the other can be accomplished using either an equation or graphic comparison scale. To convert Celsius degrees to Fahrenheit degrees, the equation is $°F = (1.8)°C + 32°$. To convert Fahrenheit degrees to Celsius degrees, the equation is $°C = (°F - 32°)/1.8$. To convert Kelvins (K) to Celsius degrees, subtract 273 and add the degree symbol.

16. Convert the following temperatures to their equivalents. Do the first four conversions using the appropriate equation, and the others using the temperature comparison scale on the inside-back cover of this manual.

   a. On a cold day it was 8°F = _____ °C

   b. Ice melts at 0°C = _____ °F

   c. Room temperature is 72°F = _____ °C

   d. A hot summer day was 35°C = _____ °F

   e. Normal body temperature is 98.6°F = _____ °C

   f. A warm shower is 27°C = _____ °F

   g. Hot soup is 72°C = _____ °F

   h. Water boils at 212°F = _____ K

17. Using the temperature comparison scale, answer the following:

   a. The thermometer reads 28°C. Will you need your winter coat? _____

   b. The thermometer reads 10°C. Will the outdoor swimming pool be open today? _____

   c. If your body temperature is 40°C, do you have a fever? _____

   d. The temperature of a cup of cocoa is 90°C. Will it burn your tongue? _____

   e. Your bath water is 15°C. Will you have a scalding, warm, or chilly bath? _____

   f. "Who's been monkeying with the thermostat? It's 37°C in this room." Are you shivering or perspiring? _____

Metric Review

Use what you have learned about the metric system to determine whether or not the following statements are *reasonable*. Write "yes" or "no" in the blanks. *Do not convert these units to English equivalents, only estimate their value.*

18. A man weighs 90 kilograms. _____

19. A fire hydrant is a meter tall. _____

20. A college student drank 3 kiloliters of coffee last night. _____

21. The room temperature is 295 K. _____

22. A dime is 1 millimeter thick. _____

23. Sugar will be sold by the milligram. _____

24. The temperature in Paris today is 80°C. _____

25. The bathtub has 80 liters of water in it. _____

26. You will need a coat if the outside temperature is 30°C. _____

27. A pork roast weighs 18 grams. _____

Special Units of Measurement

Scientists often use special units to measure various phenomena. Most of them are defined using the units of the International System of Units. Throughout this course you will encounter several of these units in your reading and laboratory studies. Only a few are introduced here.

Very Small Distances

Two units commonly used to measure very small distances are the **micrometer** (symbol, μm), also known as the **micron**, and the **nanometer** (symbol, nm).

By definition, one micrometer equals .000001 m (one millionth of a meter). There are one million micrometers in one meter and 10,000 micrometers in a centimeter. A nanometer equals .000000001 m (one billionth of a meter).

28. There are (10, 100, 1,000) nanometers in a micrometer. Circle your answer.

29. What would be the length of a 2.5 centimeter line expressed in micrometers and nanometers?

_____ micrometers in a 2.5 cm line

_____ nanometers in a 2.5 cm line

30. Some forms of *radiation* (e.g. light) travel in very small waves with distances from crest to crest of about 500 nanometers (0.5 μm). How many of these waves would it take to equal one centimeter?

_____ waves in one centimeter

Very Large Distances

On the other extreme of size, astronomers must measure very large distances, such as the distances between planets or to the stars and beyond. To simplify their measurements, they have developed special units including the **astronomical unit** (symbol, AU) and the **light-year** (symbol, LY).

The astronomical unit is a unit for measuring distance within the solar system. One astronomical unit is equal to the average distance of Earth from the Sun. This average distance is 150 million kilometers, which is approximately equal to 93 million miles.

31. The planet Saturn is 1,427 million kilometers from the Sun. How many AUs is Saturn from the Sun?

_____ AUs from the Sun

The light-year is one unit for measuring distances to the stars and beyond. One light-year is defined as the distance that light travels in a vacuum in one year. This distance is about 6 trillion miles (6,000,000,000,000 miles).

32. Approximately how many kilometers will light travel in one year?

_____ kilometers per year

33. The nearest star to Earth, excluding our Sun, is named Proxima Centauri. It is about 4.27 light-years away. What is the distance of Proxima Centauri from Earth in both miles and kilometers?

_____ miles

_____ kilometers

Density and Specific Gravity

Two important properties of a material are its **density** and **specific gravity**. Density is the mass of a substance per unit volume, usually expressed in grams per cubic centimeter (g/cm^3) in the metric system. The specific gravity of a solid is the *ratio* of the mass of a given volume of the substance to the mass of an equal volume of some other substance taken as a standard (usually water at 4°C). Because specific gravity is a ratio, it is expressed as a pure number and has no units. For example, a specific gravity of 6 means that the substance has six times more mass than an equal volume of water. Because the density of pure water at 4°C is 1 g/cm^3, the specific gravity of a substance will be numerically equal to its density.

The approximate density and specific gravity of a rock, or other solid, can be arrived at using the following steps:

Step 1: Determine the mass of the rock using a metric balance.

Step 2: Fill a graduated cylinder that has its divisions marked in milliliters approximately two-thirds full with water. Note the level of the water in the cylinder in milliliters.

Step 3: Tie a thread to the rock and immerse the rock into the water in the graduated cylinder. Note the new level of the water in the cylinder.

Step 4: Determine the difference between the beginning level and after-immersion level of the water in the cylinder.

Step 5: Calculate the density and specific gravity using the following information and appropriate equations.

A milliliter of water has a volume approximately equal to a cubic centimeter (cm^3). Therefore, the difference between the beginning water level and the after-immersion water level in the cylinder equals the volume of the rock in cubic centimeters. Furthermore, *a cubic centimeter (one milliliter) of water has a mass of approximately one gram.* (*Note:* Using the equipment already present in the lab, you may want to devise a simple experiment to confirm this fact.) Therefore, the difference between the beginning water level and the after-immersion water level in the cylinder is the mass of a volume of water equal to the volume of the rock.

Using the steps listed above for determining density and specific gravity, complete questions 34 and 35.

34. Determine the density and specific gravity of a small rock sample by completing questions 34a–34f.

a. Mass of rock sample: _____ grams

b. After-immersion level of water: _____ ml

Beginning level of water in cylinder: _____ ml

_____

Difference: _____ ml

c. Volume of rock sample: _____ cm^3

d. Mass of a volume of water equal to the volume of the rock: _____ g

e. Density of rock:

$$\text{Density} = \frac{\text{mass of rock (g)}}{\text{volume of rock (cm}^3)}$$

$$= \underline{\hspace{2cm}} \text{ g/cm}^3$$

f. Specific gravity of rock:

Specific gravity

$$= \frac{\text{mass of rock (g)}}{\text{mass of an equal volume of water (g)}}$$

$$= \underline{\hspace{1cm}}$$

35. As a means of comparison, your instructor may require that you determine the density and/or specific gravity of other objects. If so, record your results in the following spaces.

   a. Object: _____

   Density: _____ g/cm^3

   Specific gravity: _____

   b. Object: _____

   Density: _____ g/cm^3

   Specific gravity: _____

36. If you have investigated the densities and/or specific gravities of several objects, write a brief paragraph comparing the objects.

_____

_____

_____

Methods of Scientific Inquiry

Scientists use many methods in an attempt to understand natural phenomena. Some scientific discoveries represent purely theoretical ideas, while others may occasionally occur by chance. However, scientific knowledge is often gained by following a sequence of steps which involve

Step 1: Establishing a **hypothesis**—a tentative, or untested, explanation.

Step 2: Gathering data and conducting experiments to validate the hypothesis.

Step 3: Accepting, modifying, or rejecting the hypothesis on the basis of extensive data gathering or experimentation.

The following simple inquiry should help you understand the process.

Step 1—Establishing a Hypothesis

Observe all the people in the laboratory and pay particular attention to each individual's height and shoe length.

37. Based on your observations, write a hypothesis that relates a person's height to their shoe length.

   Hypothesis: _____

_____

_____

Step 2—Gathering Data

Previously, in questions 1 and 3 of the exercise, each person in the laboratory measured his or her height using a metric tape measure (or meterstick) and shoe length.

38. Gather your data by asking ten or fifteen people in the lab for their height and shoe length measurements. Enter your data in Table 3 by recording height to the nearest hundredth of a meter and shoe length to the nearest millimeter.

Step 3—Evaluating the Hypothesis Based Upon the Data

Plot all your data from Table 3 on the Height versus Shoe Length graph, Figure 5, by locating a person's height on the vertical axis and his or her shoe length on the horizontal axis. Then place a dot on the graph where the two intersect.

39. Describe the pattern of the data points (dots) on the Height versus Shoe Length graph, Figure 5. For example, are the points scattered all over the graph, or do they appear to follow a line or curve?

_____

_____

40. Draw a single line on the graph that appears to average, or best fit, the pattern of the data points.

41. Describe the relation of height to shoe length that is illustrated by the line on your graph.

_____

_____

_____

42. Ask several people, whose height and shoe length you have not used to prepare the graph, for their height. Then see how accurately your line predicts what their shoe length should be. Do this by marking each person's height on the vertical axis and then follow a line straight across to the right until you intersect the line on the

Table 3   Data Table for Recording Height and Shoe Length
Measurements of People in the Lab

Person	Height (nearest hundredth of a meter)	Shoe Length (nearest millimeter)
1	_____._____ m	_____ mm
2	_____._____ m	_____ mm
3	_____._____ m	_____ mm
4	_____._____ m	_____ mm
5	_____._____ m	_____ mm
6	_____._____ m	_____ mm
7	_____._____ m	_____ mm
8	_____._____ m	_____ mm
9	_____._____ m	_____ mm
10	_____._____ m	_____ mm
11	_____._____ m	_____ mm
12	_____._____ m	_____ mm
13	_____._____ m	_____ mm
14	_____._____ m	_____ mm
15	_____._____ m	_____ mm

graph. Read the predicted shoe length from the axis directly below the point of intersection.

43. Summarize how accurately your graph predicts a person's shoe length, knowing only his or her height.

_____

_____

_____

44. Using your graph's ability to make predictions as a guide, do you think you should accept, reject, or modify your original hypothesis? Give the reason(s) for your choice.

_____

_____

_____

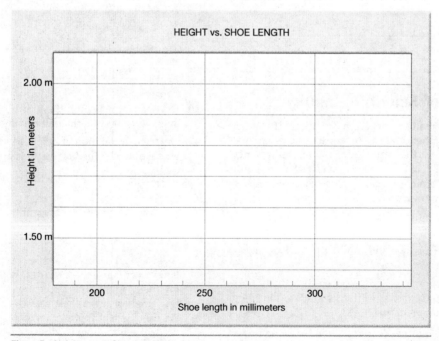

Figure 5   Height versus Shoe Length graph.

Your study has been restricted to people in your laboratory.

45. Why would your ability to make predictions have been more accurate if you had used the heights and shoe lengths of ten thousand people to construct your graph?

_____

_____

_____

Drawing hasty conclusions with limited data can often cause problems. In science you can never have too much data. Experiments are repeated many times by many different people before the results are accepted by the scientific community.

The Metric System on the Internet

Continue your analyses of the topics presented in this exercise by completing the corresponding online activity on the *Applications & Investigations in Earth Science* website at http://prenhall.com/larthsciencelab

Notes and calculations.

The Metric System, Measurements, and Scientific Inquiry

Date Due: _____

Name: _____

Date: _____

Class: _____

After you have finished this exercise, complete the following questions. You may have to refer to the exercise for assistance or to locate specific answers. Be prepared to submit this summary/report to your instructor at the designated time.

1. List the basic metric unit and symbol used for these measurements:

   Length: _____

   Mass: _____

   Volume: _____

2. Convert the following units:

   a. 2 liters = _____ deciliters

   b. 600 millimeters = _____ meter

   c. 72°F = _____ °C

   d. 0.32 kilograms = _____ grams

   e. 12 grams = _____ milligrams

3. Indicate by answering "yes" or "no" whether or not the following statements are reasonable:

   a. A person is 600 centimeters tall.

   b. A bag of groceries weighs 5 kilograms. _____

   c. It took 52 liters of gasoline to fill the car's empty gasoline tank. _____

4. List your height and shoe length using the metric system.

   a. Height: _____ . _____ meters

   b. Shoe length: _____ millimeters

5. How many micrometers are there in 3.0 centimeters?

   _____ micrometers in 3.0 centimeters

6. How many waves, each 500 nanometers wide, would fit along a two centimeter line?

   _____ waves along a two centimeter line

7. What would be the distance in kilometers of a star that is 6.5 light-years from Earth?

   _____ kilometers from Earth

8. Uranus, one of the most distant planets, is 2,870 million kilometers from the Sun. What is its distance from the Sun in astronomical units?

   _____ astronomical units from the Sun

9. Explain the difference between the two terms, *density* and *specific gravity*.

   _____

   _____

   _____

10. At the conclusion of your height–shoe length experiment, in question 44 you (accepted, rejected, modified) your original hypothesis. Circle your answer and give the reason for this decision.

    _____

    _____

    _____

Location and Distance on Earth

The ability to find places and features on Earth's surface using maps and globes is an essential skill required of all Earth scientists. This exercise introduces the most commonly used system for determining location on Earth. Using the system as a foundation, you will examine ways to measure distance on Earth's surface.

Objectives

After you have completed this exercise, you should be able to:

1. Explain the most common system used for locating places and features on Earth.
2. Use Earth's grid system to accurately locate a place or feature.
3. Explain the relation between latitude and the angle of the North Star (Polaris) above the horizon.
4. Explain the relation between longitude and solar time.
5. Determine the shortest route and distance between any two places on Earth's surface.

Materials

ruler   calculator
protractor

Materials Supplied by Your Instructor

globe   50–80 cm length of
world wall map   string
atlas

Terms

Earth's grid	South Pole	solar time
latitude	longitude	standard time
parallel of	meridian of	great circle
latitude	longitude	small circle
equator	prime meridian	
North Pole	hemisphere	

Introduction

Globes and maps each have a system of north–south and east–west lines, called the **Earth's grid**, that forms the basis for locating points on Earth (Figure 1). The grid is, in effect, much like a large sheet of graph paper that has been laid over the surface of Earth. Using the system is very similar to using a graph; that is, the position of a point is determined by the intersection of two lines.

   Latitude is north–south distance on Earth (Figure 1). The lines (circles) of the grid that extend around Earth in an east–west direction are called **parallels of latitude**. *Parallels of latitude mark north and south distance from the* **equator** *on Earth's surface.* As their name implies, these circles are parallel to one another. Two places on Earth, the **North Pole** and **South Pole**, are exceptions; they are points of latitude rather than circles.

   Longitude is east–west distance on Earth (Figure 1). **Meridians of longitude** are each halves of circles that extend from the North Pole to the South Pole on

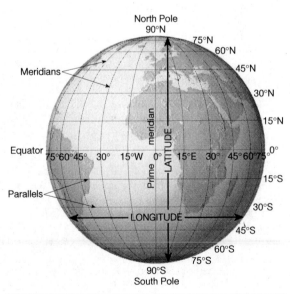

Figure 1 Earth's grid system.

one side of Earth. *Meridians of longitude mark east and west distance from the **prime meridian** on Earth's surface.* Adjacent meridians are farthest apart on the equator and converge (come together) toward the poles.

> **The intersection of a parallel of latitude with a meridian of longitude determines the location of a point on Earth's surface.**

Earth's shape is nearly spherical. Since parallels and meridians mark distances on a sphere, their designation, like distance around a circle, is given in *degrees* (°). For more precise location, a degree can be subdivided into sixty equal parts, called *minutes* ('), and a minute of angle can be divided into sixty parts, called *seconds* ("). Thus, 31°10'20" means 31 degrees, 10 minutes, and 20 seconds.

The type of map or globe used determines the accuracy to which a place may be located. On detailed maps it is often possible to estimate latitude and longitude to the nearest degree, minute, and second. On the other hand, when using a world map or globe, it may only be possible to estimate latitude and longitude to the nearest whole degree or two.

In addition to showing location on Earth, latitude and longitude can be used to determine distance. Knowing the shape and size of Earth, the distance in miles and kilometers covered by a degree of latitude or longitude has been calculated. These measurements provide the foundation for navigation.

Determining Latitude

The equator is a circle drawn on a globe that is equally distant from both the North Pole and South Pole. It divides the globe into two equal halves, called **hemispheres**. The equator serves as the beginning point for determining latitude and is assigned the value 0°00'00" latitude.

> **Latitude is distance north and south of the equator, measured as an angle in degrees from the center of Earth (Figure 2).**

Latitude begins at the equator, extends north to the North Pole, designated 90°00'00"N latitude (a 90° angle measured north from the equator), and also extends south to the South Pole, designated 90°00'00"S latitude. *The poles and all parallels of latitude, with the exception of the equator, are designated either N (if they are north of the equator) or S (if they are south of the equator).*

1. Locate the equator on a globe. Figure 3 represents Earth, with point B its center. Sketch and label the equator on the diagram in Figure 3. Also label the Northern Hemisphere and Southern Hemisphere on the diagram.

2. On Figure 3, make an angle by drawing a line from point A on the equator to point B (the center

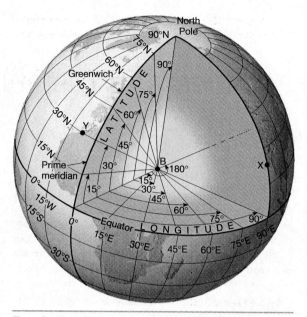

Figure 2   Measuring latitude and longitude. The angle measured from the equator to the center of Earth (B) and then northward to the parallel where point Y is located is 30°. Therefore, the latitude of point Y is 30°N. All points on the same parallel as Y are designated 30°N latitude.

   The angle measured from the prime meridian where it crosses the equator to the center of Earth (B) and then eastward to the meridian where point X is located, is 90°. Therefore, the longitude of point X is 90°E. All points on the same meridian as X are designated 90°E longitude.

of Earth). Then extend the line from point B to point C in the Northern Hemisphere. The angle you have drawn (∠ABC) is 45°. Therefore, by definition of latitude, point C is at 45°N latitude.

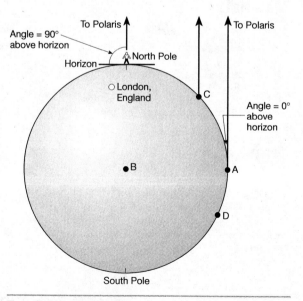

Figure 3   Hypothetical Earth.

3. Draw a line on Figure 3 parallel to the equator that also goes through point C. All points on this line are 45°N latitude.

4. Using a protractor, measure ∠ABD on Figure 3. Then draw a line parallel to the equator that also goes through point D. Label the line with its proper latitude.

On a map or globe, parallels may be drawn at any interval.

5. How many degrees of latitude separate the parallels on the globe you are using?

_____ degrees of latitude between each parallel

6. Keep in mind that the lines (circles) of latitude are parallel to the equator and to each other. Locate some other parallels on the globe. Sketch and label a few of these on Figure 3.

7. Use the diagram that illustrates parallels of latitude, Figure 4, to answer questions 7a and 7b.

   a. Accurately draw and label the following additional parallels of latitude on the figure.

   5°N latitude

   10°S latitude

   25°N latitude

   b. Refer to Figure 4. Write out the latitude for each designated point as was done for points A and B. Remember to indicate whether the point is north or south of the equator by writing an N or S and include the word "latitude."

   Point A: (30°N latitude)   Point D: _____

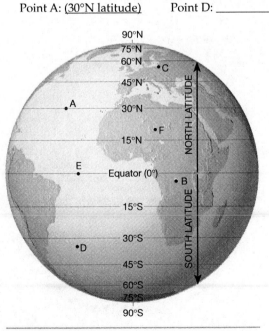

Figure 4 Parallels of latitude.

Point B: (5°S latitude)   Point E: _____

Point C: _____   Point F: _____

8. Use a globe or atlas to locate the cities listed below and give their latitude to the nearest degree. Indicate N or S and include the word "latitude."

   Moscow, Russia: _____

   Durban, South Africa: _____

   Your home city: _____

   Your college campus city: _____

9. By using a globe or atlas, give the name of a city or feature that is equally as far south of the equator as your home city is north.

   _____

10. The farthest one can be from the equator is (45, 90, 180) degrees of latitude. Circle your answer.

11. The two places on Earth that are farthest from the equator to the north and to the south are called the

   _____ and _____.

There are five special parallels of latitude marked and named on most globes.

12. Use a globe or atlas to locate the following special parallels and indicate the name given to each.

                                    NAME OF PARALLEL

   66°30′00″N latitude: _____

   23°30′00″N latitude: _____

   0°00′00″ latitude: _____

   23°30′00″S latitude: _____

   66°30′00″S latitude: _____

Latitude and the North Star

Today most ships use GPS navigational satellites to determine their location. (For information about the Global Positioning System, visit the website listed at the end of this exercise.) However, early explorers were well aware of the concept of latitude and could use the angle of the North Star (a star named Polaris) above the horizon to determine their north–south position in the Northern Hemisphere. As shown on Figure 3, someone standing at the North Pole would look overhead (90° angle above the horizon) to see Polaris. Their latitude is 90°00′00″N. On the other hand, someone standing on the equator, 0°00′00″ latitude, would observe Polaris on the horizon (0° angle above the horizon).

Use Figure 3 to answer questions 13–14.

13. The angle of Polaris above the horizon for some-one standing at point C would be (45°, 90°, 180°). Circle your answer.

14. What is the relation between a particular latitude and the angle of Polaris above the horizon at that latitude?

_____

15. What is the angle of Polaris above the horizon at the following cities?

ANGLE OF POLARIS
ABOVE THE HORIZON

Fairbanks, AK: _____ degrees

St. Paul, MN: _____ degrees

New Orleans, LA: _____ degrees

Your home city: _____ degrees

Your college campus city: _____ degrees

Determining Longitude

Meridians are the north–south lines (half circles) on the globe that converge at the poles and are farthest apart along the equator. They are used to determine longitude, which is distance east and west on Earth (Figure 1). Each meridian extends from pole to pole on one side of the globe.

Notice on the globe that all meridians are alike. The choice of a zero, or beginning, meridian was arbitrary. The meridian that was chosen by international agreement in 1884 to be 0°00′00″ longitude passes through the Royal Astronomical Observatory at Greenwich, England, located near London. This internationally accepted reference for longitude is named the *prime meridian*.

> Longitude is distance, measured as an angle in degrees east and west of the prime meridian (Figure 2).

Longitude begins at the prime meridian (0°00′00″ longitude) and extends to the east and to the west, halfway around Earth to the 180°00′00″ meridian, which is directly opposite the prime meridian. *All meridians, with the exception of the prime meridian and the 180° meridian, are designated either E (if they are east of the prime meridian) or W (if they are west of the prime meridian).*

16. Locate the prime meridian on a globe. Sketch and label it on the diagram of Earth, Figure 3.

17. Label the Eastern Hemisphere, that half of the globe with longitudes east of the prime meridian, and the Western Hemisphere on Figure 3.

On a map or globe, meridians can be drawn at any interval.

18. How many degrees of longitude separate each of the meridians on your globe?

_____ degrees of longitude between each meridian

19. Keep in mind that meridians are farthest apart at the equator and converge at the poles. Sketch and label several meridians on Figure 3.

20. Use the diagram that illustrates meridians of longitude, Figure 5, to answer questions 20a and 20b.

   a. Accurately draw and label the following additional meridians of longitude on the figure.
      35°W longitude
      70°E longitude
      10°W longitude

   b. Refer to Figure 5. Write out the longitude for each designated point as was done for points A and B. Remember to indicate whether the point is east or west of the prime meridian by writing an E or W and include the word "longitude."

      Point A: (30°E longitude)   Point D: _____

      Point B: (20°W longitude)   Point E: _____

      Point C: _____   Point F: _____

21. Use a globe or atlas to locate the cities listed below and give their longitude to the nearest degree. Indicate either E or W and include the word "longitude."

   Wellington, New Zealand: _____

   Honolulu, Hawaii: _____

   Your home city: _____

   Your college campus city: _____

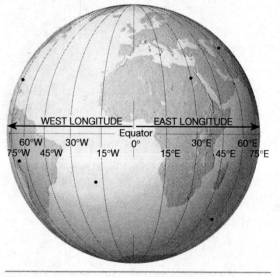

Figure 5 Meridians of longitude.

22. Using a globe or atlas, give the name of a city, feature, or country that is at the same latitude as your home city but equally distant from the prime meridian in the opposite hemisphere.

_____

23. The farthest a place can be directly east or west of the prime meridian is (45, 90, 180) degrees of longitude. Circle your answer.

Longitude and Time

Time, while independent of latitude, is very much related to longitude. This fact allows for time to be used in navigation to accurately determine one's location. By knowing the difference in time between two places, one with known longitude, the longitude of the second place can be determined.

Time on Earth can be kept in two ways. **Solar**, or **Sun, time** uses the position of the Sun in the sky to determine time. **Standard time**, the system used throughout most of the world, divides the globe into 24 standard time zones. Everyone living within the same standard time zone keeps the clock set the same. Of the two, solar time is used to determine longitude.

The following basic facts are important to understanding time.

- Earth rotates on its axis from west to east (eastward) or counterclockwise when viewed from above the North Pole (Figure 6).

- It is noon, Sun time, on the meridian that is directly facing the Sun (the Sun has reached its highest position in the sky, called the _zenith_) and midnight on the meridian on the opposite side of Earth.

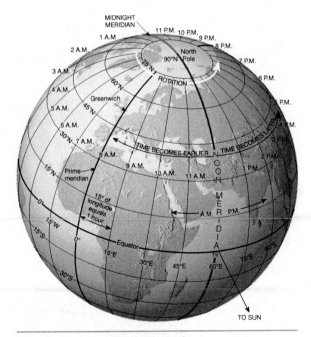

Figure 6 The noon meridian and solar time.

- The time interval from one noon by the Sun to the next noon averages 24 hours and is known as the _mean solar day_.

- Earth turns through 360° of longitude in one mean solar day, which is equivalent to 15° of longitude per hour or 1° of longitude every 4 minutes of time.

- Places that are east or west of each other, regardless of the distance, have different solar times. For example, people located to the east of the noon meridian have already experienced noon; their time is afternoon [P.M.—_post_ (after) _meridiem_ (the noon meridian)]. People living west of the noon meridian have yet to reach noon; their time is before noon [A.M.—_ante_ (before) _meridiem_ (the noon meridian)]. _Time becomes later going eastward and earlier going westward._

Use the basic facts of time to answer questions 24–26.

24. What would be the solar time of a person living 1° of longitude west of the noon meridian? Be sure to indicate A.M. or P.M. with your answer.

Solar time: _____ (A.M., P.M.)

25. What would be the solar time of a person located 4° of longitude east of the noon meridian?

Solar time: _____ (A.M., P.M.)

26. If it is noon, solar time, at 70°W longitude, what is the solar time at each of the following locations?

	SOLAR TIME
72°W longitude:	_____
65°W longitude:	_____
90°W longitude:	_____
110°E longitude:	_____

Early navigators had to wait for the invention of accurate clocks, called _chronometers_, before they could determine longitude. Today most navigation is done using satellites, but ships still carry chronometers as a backup system.

The shipboard chronometer is set to keep the time at a known place on Earth, for example, the prime meridian. If it is noon by the Sun where the ship is located, and at that same instant the chronometer indicates that it is 8 A.M. on the prime meridian, the ship must be 60° of longitude (4 hours difference × 15° per hour) east (the ship's time is later) of the prime meridian (Figure 6). The difference in time need not be in whole hours. Thirty minutes difference in time between two places would be equivalent to 7.5° of longitude, twenty minutes would equal 5°, and so forth.

27. It is exactly noon by the Sun at a ship's location. What is the ship's longitude if, at that instant, the time on the prime meridian is the following? (_Note:_ Drawing a diagram showing the prime meridian, the ship's location east or west of the prime meridian, and the difference in hours may be helpful.)

6:00 P.M.: _____

1:00 A.M.: _____

2:30 P.M.: _____

Using Earth's Grid System

Using both parallels of latitude and meridians of longitude, you can accurately locate any point on the surface of Earth.

28. Using Figure 7, determine the latitude and longitude of each of the lettered points and write your answers in the following spaces. As a guide, Point A has already been done. Remember to indicate whether the point is N or S latitude and E or W longitude. The only exceptions are the equator, prime meridian, and 180° meridian. They are given no direction because each is a single line and cannot be confused with any other line. Convention dictates that latitude is always listed first.

Point A: <u>(30°N)</u> latitude,   <u>(60°E)</u> longitude

Point B: _____ latitude,   _____ longitude

Point C: _____ latitude,   _____ longitude

Point D: _____ latitude,   _____ longitude

Point E: _____ latitude,   _____ longitude

29. Locate the following points on Figure 7. Place a dot on the figure at the proper location and label each point with the designated letter.

Point F: 15°S latitude, 75°W longitude

Point G: 45°N latitude, 0° longitude

Point H: 30°S latitude, 60°E longitude

Point I: 0° latitude, 30°E longitude

30. Use a globe, map, or atlas to determine the latitude and longitude of the following cities.

Kansas City, MO: _____

Miami, FL: _____

Oslo, Norway: _____

Auckland, New Zealand: _____

Quito, Ecuador: _____

Baghdad, Iraq: _____

31. Beginning with a globe or world wall map, and then proceeding to an atlas, determine the city or feature at the following locations.

19°28'N latitude, 99°09'W longitude:

_____

41°52'N latitude, 12°37'E longitude:

_____

1°30'S latitude, 33°00'E longitude:

_____

When you study the Earth sciences, it is important to be familiar with the major physical features of Earth's surface. Identifying the features on a map will help acquaint you with their location for future reference.

32. Use a wall map of the world or world map in an atlas to find the following water bodies, rivers, and mountains. Examine their latitudes and longitudes, and then label each on the world map, Figure 8. To conserve space, mark only the num-

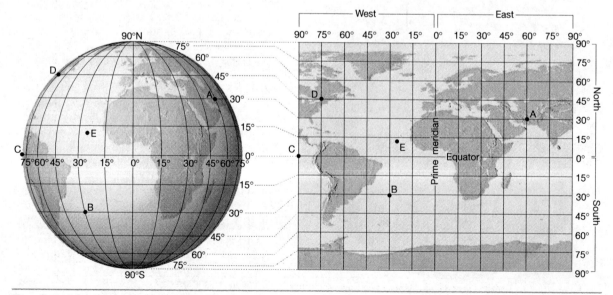

Figure 7 Locating places using Earth's grid system.

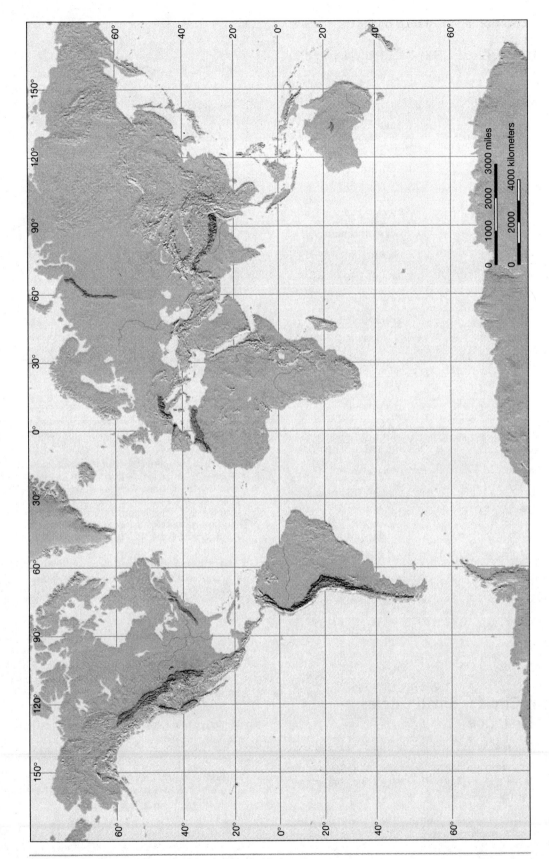

Figure 8 Generalized world map showing select physical features.

19

ber or letter of the feature at the appropriate location on the map.

Water Bodies

A. Pacific Ocean

B. Atlantic Ocean

C. Indian Ocean

D. Arctic Ocean

E. Gulf of Mexico

F. Mediterranean Sea

G. Caribbean Sea

H. Persian Gulf

I. Red Sea

J. Sea of Japan

K. Black Sea

L. Caspian Sea

Rivers

North America

a. Mississippi

b. Colorado

c. Missouri

d. Ohio

South America

e. Amazon

Europe and Asia

f. Volga

g. Mekong

h. Ganges

i. Yangtze

Africa and Australia

j. Nile

k. Congo

l. Darling

Mountains

North America

1. Rocky Mountains

2. Cascade Range

3. Sierra Nevada

4. Appalachian
     Mountains

5. Black Hills

6. Teton Range

7. Adirondack
     Mountains

South America

8. Andes Mountains

Europe and Asia

9. Pyrenees Mountains

10. Alps

11. Himalaya Mountains

12. Ural Mountains

Africa and Australia

13. Atlas Mountains

14. MacDonnell Ranges

Great Circles, Small Circles, and Distance

Great Circles

A **great circle** is the largest possible circle that can be drawn on a globe (Figure 9). Some of the characteristics of a great circle are

- A great circle divides the globe into two equal parts, called *hemispheres*.
- An infinite number of great circles can be drawn on a globe. Therefore, a great circle can be drawn that passes through any two places on Earth's surface.

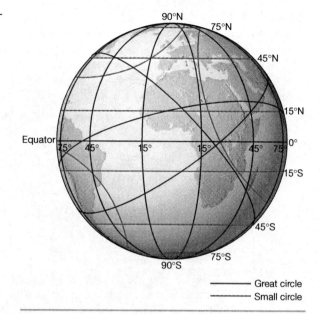

Figure 9   Illustrated are a few of the infinite number of great circles and small circles that can be drawn on the globe.

- The shortest distance between two places on Earth is along the great circle that passes through those two places.
- If Earth were a perfect sphere, then one degree of angle along a great circle would cover an identical distance everywhere. Because Earth is slightly flattened at the *poles and bulges slightly* at the equator, there are small differences in the length of a degree. However, for most purposes, *one degree of angle along a great circle equals approximately 111 kilometers or 69 miles.*

Referring to Figure 9 and keeping the characteristics of great circles in mind, examine a globe and answer questions 33–35.

33. Remember that great circles do not necessarily have to follow parallels or meridians. Estimate several great circles on the globe. Do this by wrapping a piece of string around the globe that divides the globe into two equal halves. You should be able to see that there are an infinite number of great circles that can be marked on the globe.

34. Which parallel(s) of latitude is/are a great circle(s)?

_____

Meridians of longitude are each half circles. If each meridian is paired with the meridian on the opposite side of the globe, a circle is formed.

35. Which meridians that have been paired with their opposite meridian on the globe are great circles?

_____

Small Circles

Any circle on the globe that does not meet the characteristics of a great circle is considered a **small circle** (Figure 9). Therefore, a small circle *does not* divide the globe into two equal parts and *is not* the shortest distance between two places on Earth. Referring to Figure 9 and keeping the characteristics of small circles in mind, examine a globe and answer questions 36–38.

36. In general, which parallels of latitude are small circles?

_____

37. Which two latitudes are actually points, rather than circles?

_____

38. In general, which meridians that have been paired with their opposite meridian on the globe are small circles?

_____

39. Indicate, by placing an "X" in the appropriate column, which of the following pairs of points illustrated on the Earth's grid in Figure 7 are on a great circle and which are on a small circle.

	GREAT CIRCLE	SMALL CIRCLE
Points A–H	_____	_____
Points D–G	_____	_____
Points C–I	_____	_____
Points B–H	_____	_____

40. Now that you know the characteristics of great and small circles, complete the following statements by circling the correct response.

a. All meridians are halves of (great, small) circles.

b. With the exception of the equator, all parallels are (great, small) circles.

c. The equator is a (great, small) circle.

d. The poles are (points, lines) of latitude, rather than circles.

Determining Distance Along a Great Circle

Determining the distance between two places on Earth when both are on the equator or the same great circle meridian requires two steps:

Step 1: Determine the number of degrees along the great circle between the two places (degrees of longitude on the equator or degrees of latitude on a meridian).

Step 2: Multiply the number of degrees by 111 kilometers or 69 miles (the approximate number of kilometers or miles per degree for any great circle).

Use a globe and these steps to answer questions 41 and 42.

41. Approximately how many miles would you journey if you traveled from 10°W longitude to 40°E longitude at the equator by way of the shortest route?

_____ miles

42. Approximately how many kilometers is London, England, directly north of the equator?

_____ kilometers

Determining the shortest distance between two places on Earth that are *not* both on the equator or the same great circle meridian requires the four steps (Figure 10):

Step 1: On a globe, determine the great circle that intersects both places.

Step 2: Stretch a piece of string along the great circle between the two places on the globe and mark the distance between them on the string with your fingers (Figure 10A).

Step 3: While still marking the distance with your fingers, place the string on the equator with one end on the prime meridian. Determine the number of degrees along the great circle between the two places by measuring the marked string's length in degrees of longitude along the equator, which is also a great circle (Figure 10B).

Step 4: Multiply the number of degrees along the great circle by 69 miles (111 kilometers) to arrive at the approximate distance. (For example, the great circle distance between X and Y in Figure 10 would be approximately 2,070 miles, 30° × 69 miles/degree, or 3330 kilometers, 30° × 111 kilometers/degree.)

Use a globe, a piece of string, and the four steps to answer questions 43 and 44.

43. Determine the approximate great circle distance in degrees, miles, and kilometers from Memphis, Tennessee, to Tokyo, Japan.

Degrees along the great circle between Memphis and Tokyo = _____°

Distance along the great circle between Memphis and Tokyo = _____ miles (_____ km)

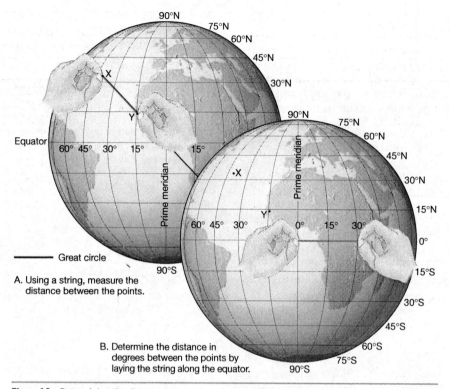

A. Using a string, measure the distance between the points.

— Great circle

B. Determine the distance in degrees between the points by laying the string along the equator.

Figure 10   Determining the distance between two places on Earth along a great circle other than the equator or great circle meridian. In the example illustrated, the distance between X and Y along the great circle is 30°, which is approximately equivalent to 2,070 miles (3,330 kilometers).

44. Describe the flight route, by listing states, countries, etc., that a plane would follow as it flew by way of the shortest route between Memphis, Tennessee, and Tokyo, Japan.

_____

_____

Determining Distance Along a Parallel

Since all parallels except the equator are small circles, the length of one degree of longitude along a parallel, other than the equator, will always be less than 69 miles or 111 kilometers. Table 1 shows the length of a degree of longitude at various latitudes on Earth.

45. Examine a globe. What do you observe about the distance around Earth along each parallel as you get farther away from the equator?

_____

46. Use Table 1, "Longitude as distance," to determine the length of one degree of longitude at each of the following parallels.

LENGTH OF 1° OF LONGITUDE

15° latitude: _____ km, _____ miles

30° latitude: _____ km, _____ miles

45° latitude: _____ km, _____ miles

80° latitude: _____ km, _____ miles

47. Use the Earth's grid illustrated in Figure 7 to determine the distances between the following points.

Distance between points D and G:

_____ degrees × _____ miles/degree

= _____ miles

Distance between points B and H:

_____ degrees × _____ km/degree

= _____ km

Memphis, Tennessee, and Tokyo, Japan, are both located at about 35°N latitude.

48. Use a globe or world map to determine how many degrees of longitude separate Memphis, Tennessee, from Tokyo, Japan.

Table 1   Longitude as Distance

°Lat.	Length of 1° Long. km	Length of 1° Long. miles	°Lat.	Length of 1° Long. km	Length of 1° Long. miles	°Lat.	Length of 1° Long. km	Length of 1° Long. miles
0	111.367	69.172	30	96.528	59.955	60	55.825	34.674
1	111.349	69.161	31	95.545	59.345	61	54.131	33.622
2	111.298	69.129	32	94.533	58.716	62	52.422	32.560
3	111.214	69.077	33	93.493	58.070	63	50.696	31.488
4	111.096	69.004	34	92.425	57.407	64	48.954	30.406
5	110.945	68.910	35	91.327	56.725	65	47.196	29.314
6	110.760	68.795	36	90.203	56.027	66	45.426	28.215
7	110.543	68.660	37	89.051	55.311	67	43.639	27.105
8	110.290	68.503	38	87.871	54.578	68	41.841	25.988
9	110.003	68.325	39	86.665	53.829	69	40.028	24.862
10	109.686	68.128	40	85.431	53.063	70	38.204	23.729
11	109.333	67.909	41	84.171	52.280	71	36.368	22.589
12	108.949	67.670	42	82.886	51.482	72	34.520	21.441
13	108.530	67.410	43	81.575	50.668	73	32.662	20.287
14	108.079	67.130	44	80.241	49.839	74	30.793	19.126
15	107.596	66.830	45	78.880	48.994	75	28.914	17.959
16	107.079	66.509	46	77.497	48.135	76	27.029	16.788
17	106.530	66.168	47	76.089	47.260	77	25.134	15.611
18	105.949	65.807	48	74.659	46.372	78	23.229	14.428
19	105.337	65.427	49	73.203	45.468	79	21.320	13.242
20	104.692	65.026	50	71.727	44.551	80	19.402	12.051
21	104.014	64.605	51	70.228	43.620	81	17.480	10.857
22	103.306	64.165	52	68.708	42.676	82	15.551	9.659
23	102.565	63.705	53	67.168	41.719	83	13.617	8.458
24	101.795	63.227	54	65.604	40.748	84	11.681	7.255
25	100.994	62.729	55	64.022	39.765	85	9.739	6.049
26	100.160	62.211	56	62.420	38.770	86	7.796	4.842
27	99.297	61.675	57	60.798	37.763	87	5.849	3.633
28	98.405	61.121	58	59.159	36.745	88	3.899	2.422
29	97.481	60.547	59	57.501	35.715	89	1.950	1.211
30	96.528	59.955	60	55.825	34.674	90	0.000	0.000

_____ degrees of longitude separate Memphis, Tennessee, and Tokyo, Japan.

49. From the longitude as distance table, Table 1, the length of one degree of longitude at latitude 35°N is

_____ km (_____ miles).

50. How many miles is Tokyo, Japan, *directly* west of Memphis, TN? Show your calculation below.

_____ miles

51. In question 43 you determined the great circle distance between Memphis, Tennessee, and

Tokyo, Japan. How many miles shorter is the great circle route between these cities than the east–west distance along a parallel (question 50)?

The great circle route is _____ miles shorter.

Location and Distance on Earth on the Internet

Continue your analyses of the topics presented in this exercise by completing the corresponding online activity on the *Applications & Investigations in Earth Science* website at http://prenhall.com/earthsciencelab

Notes and calculations.

Location and Distance on Earth

Date Due: _____

Name: _____

Date: _____

Class: _____

After you have finished this exercise, complete the following questions. You may have to refer to the exercise for assistance or to locate specific answers. Be prepared to submit this summary/report to your instructor at the designated time.

1. In Figure 11, prepare a diagram illustrating Earth's grid system. Include and label the equator and prime meridian. Refer to the diagram to explain the system used for locating points on the surface of Earth.

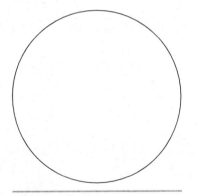

Figure 11 Diagram of Earth's grid system.

Explanation: _____

_____

_____

2. Define the following terms.

Parallel of latitude: _____

_____

Meridian of longitude: _____

_____

Great circle: _____

_____

3. Determine whether or not the following statements are true or false. If the statement is false, correct the word(s) so that it reads as a true statement.

T F a. The distance measured north or south of the prime meridian is called latitude.

T F b. All meridians, when paired with their opposite meridian on Earth, form great circles.

T F c. The equator is the only meridian that is a great circle.

4. What is the relation between the latitude of a place in the Northern Hemisphere and the angle of Polaris above the horizon at that place?

_____

5. Approximately how many miles does one degree equal along a great circle?

One degree along a great circle equals _____ miles.

6. What is the latitude and longitude of your home city?

_____ latitude, _____ longitude

7. Use a globe or map to determine, as accurately as possible, the latitude and longitude of Athens, Greece.

_____ latitude, _____ longitude

8. Write a brief paragraph describing how to determine the shortest distance between two places on Earth's surface.

_____

_____

_____

9. From question 51 of the exercise, how many miles shorter is the great circle route between Memphis, Tennessee, and Tokyo, Japan, than the straight east–west distance along a parallel?

   _____ miles shorter

10. Approximately how many miles is it from London, England, to the South Pole? (Show your calculation.)

    _____ miles

11. Using Figure 12, determine the latitude and longitude of each of the lettered points and write your answers in the following spaces.

    Point A: _____

    Point B: _____

    Point C: _____

    Point D: _____

    Point E: _____

12. You are shipwrecked and floating in the Atlantic Ocean somewhere between London, England, and New York, New York. Fortunately, you managed to save your globe. You have been in London so your watch is still set for London time. It is noon, by the Sun, at your location. Your watch indicates that it is 4 P.M. in London. Are you closer to the United States or to England? Explain how you arrived at your answer.

_____

_____

_____

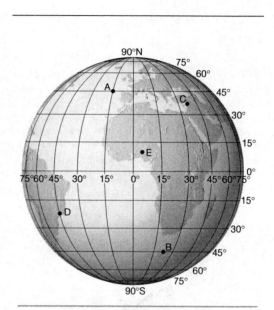

Figure 12   Locating places using Earth's grid.

Earth–Sun Relations

To life on this planet, the relations between Earth and the Sun are perhaps the most important of all astronomical phenomena. The variations in solar energy striking Earth as it rotates and revolves around the Sun cause the seasons and therefore are an appropriate starting point for studying weather and climate.

In this exercise you will investigate the reasons why the amount of solar radiation intercepted by Earth varies for different latitudes and changes throughout the year at a particular place (Figure 1).

Objectives

After you have completed this exercise, you should be able to:

1. Describe the effect that Sun angle has on the amount of solar radiation a place receives.
2. Explain why the intensity and duration of solar radiation varies with latitude.
3. Explain why the intensity and duration of solar radiation varies at any one place throughout the year.
4. Describe the significance of these special parallels of latitude: Tropic of Cancer, Tropic of Capricorn, Arctic Circle, Antarctic Circle, and equator.
5. Diagram the relation between Earth and the Sun on the dates of the solstices and equinoxes.
6. Determine the latitude where the overhead Sun is located on any day of the year.
7. Calculate the noon Sun angle for any place on Earth on any day.
8. Calculate the latitude of a place using the noon Sun angle.

Materials

metric ruler   colored pencils
protractor   calculator

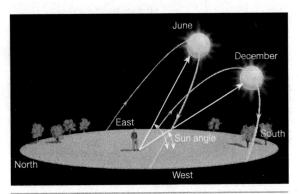

Figure 1 Daily paths of the Sun for June and December for an observer in the middle latitudes in the Northern Hemisphere. Notice that the angle of the Sun above the horizon is much greater in the summer than in the winter.

Materials Supplied by Your Instructor

globe
large rubber band or string

Terms

weather	solar constant	solstice
weather element	equator	equinox
weather control	Tropic of Cancer	analemma
solar intensity	Tropic of Capricorn	noon Sun
solar duration	Arctic Circle	angle
langley	Antarctic Circle	
calorie		

Introduction

Weather is the state of the atmosphere at a particular place for a short period of time. The condition of the atmosphere at any location and time is described by measuring the four basic **elements** of weather: temperature, moisture, air pressure, and wind. Of all the **controls** that are responsible for causing variations in the weather elements, the amount of solar radiation received at any location is the most important.

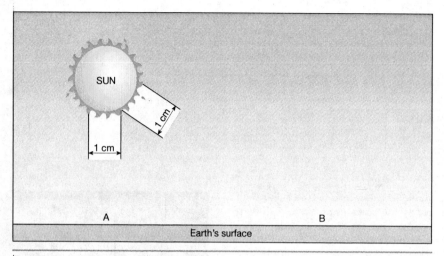

Figure 2   Vertical and oblique Sun beams.

Solar Radiation and the Seasons

The amount of solar energy (radiation) striking the outer edge of the atmosphere is not uniform over the face of Earth at any one time, nor is it constant throughout the year at any particular place. Rather, solar radiation at any location and time is determined by the Sun's **intensity** and **duration**. Intensity is the angle at which the rays of sunlight strike a surface, whereas duration refers to the length of daylight.

The standard unit of solar radiation is the **langley**, equal to one **calorie**[1] per square centimeter. The **solar constant**, or average intensity of solar radiation falling on a surface perpendicular to the solar beam at the outer edge of the atmosphere, is about 2 langleys per minute. As the radiation passes through the atmosphere, it undergoes absorption, reflection, and scattering. Therefore, at any one location, less radiation reaches Earth's surface than was originally intercepted at the upper atmosphere.

Solar Radiation and Latitude

The amount of radiation striking a square meter at the outer edge of the atmosphere, and eventually Earth's surface, varies with latitude because of a changing Sun angle (see Figure 1). To illustrate this fact, answer questions 1–11 using the appropriate figure.

1. On Figure Table 2, extend the 1-cm-wide beam of sunlight from the Sun vertically to point A on the

[1]The most familiar energy unit used to measure heat is the calorie, which is the quantity of heat energy needed to raise the temperature of one gram of water one degree Celsius. Do not confuse it with the so-called large Calorie (note the capital C), the kind counted by weight watchers. A Calorie is the amount of heat energy needed to raise the temperature of a kilogram (1,000 grams) of water 1 degree Celsius.

surface. Extend the second 1-cm-wide beam, beginning at the Sun, to the surface at point B.

Notice in Figure 2 that the Sun is directly overhead (vertical) at point A and the beam of sunlight strikes the surface at a 90° angle above the horizon.

Using Figure 2, answer questions 2–5.

2. Using a protractor, measure the angle between the surface and the beam of sunlight coming from the Sun to point B.

   _____° = angle of the Sun above the surface (horizon) at point B.

3. What are the lengths of the line segments on the surface covered by the Sun beam at point A and point B?

   Point A: _____ mm   point B: _____ mm

4. Of the two beams, beam (A, B) is more spread out at the surface and covers a larger area. Circle your answer.

5. More langleys per minute would be received by a square centimeter on the surface at point (A, B). Circle your answer.

Use Figure 3 to answer questions 6–11 concerning the total amount of solar radiation intercepted by each 30° segment of latitude on Earth.

6. With a metric ruler, measure the total width of incoming rays from point x to point y in Figure 3. The total width is _____ centimeters (_____ millimeters). Fill in your answers.

7. Assume the total width of the incoming rays from point x to point y equals 100% of the solar radiation that is intercepted by Earth. Each cen-

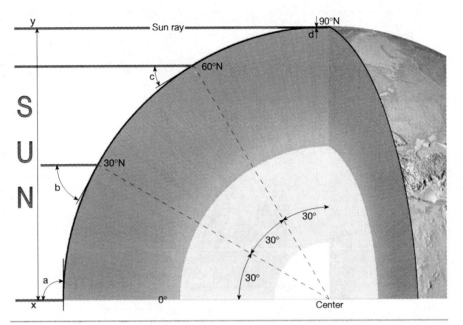

Figure 3 Distribution of solar radiation per 30° segment of latitude on Earth.

timeter would equal _____%, and each millimeter would equal _____%. Fill in your answers.

8. What percentage of the total incoming radiation is concentrated in each of the following zones?

0°–30° = _____ mm = _____ %

30°–60° = _____ mm = _____ %

60°–90° = _____ mm = _____ %

9. Use a protractor to measure the angle between the surface and Sun ray at each of the following locations. (Angle b is already done as an example.)

Angle a: _____ °   angle c: _____ °

Angle b: ___60°___   angle d: _____ °

10. What is the general relation between the amount of radiation received in each 30° segment and the angle of the Sun's rays?

_____

_____

11. Explain in your own words what fact about Earth creates the unequal distribution of solar energy, even though each zone represents an equal 30° segment of latitude.

_____

_____

_____

Yearly Variation in Solar Energy

The amount of solar radiation received at a particular place would remain constant throughout the year if it were not for these facts:

- Earth rotates on its axis and revolves around the Sun.
- The axis of Earth is inclined 23.5° from the perpendicular to the plane of its orbit.
- Throughout the year, the axis of Earth points to the same place in the sky, which causes the overhead (vertical or 90°) noon Sun to cross over the **equator** twice as it migrates from the **Tropic of Cancer** (23.5°N latitude) to the **Tropic of Capricorn** (23.5°S latitude) and back to the Tropic of Cancer.

As a consequence, the position of the vertical or overhead noon Sun shifts between the hemispheres, causing variations in the intensity of solar radiation and changes in the length of daylight and darkness. *The seasons are the result of this changing intensity and duration of solar energy and subsequent heating of the atmosphere.*

To help understand how the intensity and duration of solar radiation varies throughout the year, answer questions 12–31 after you have examined the location of the Tropic of Cancer, Tropic of Capricorn, **Arctic Circle**, and **Antarctic Circle** on a globe or world map.

12. List some of the countries each of the following special parallels of latitude passes through.

Tropic of Cancer:_____

Tropic of Capricorn: _____

Arctic Circle: _____

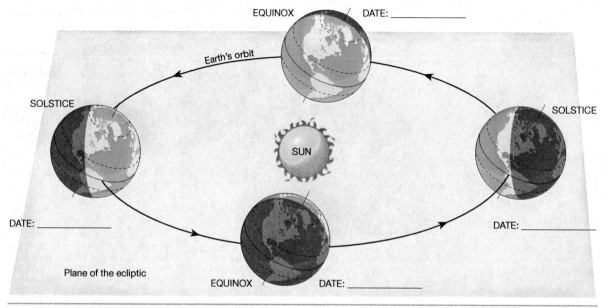

Figure 4   Earth–Sun relations.

13. Write the date represented by each position of Earth at the appropriate place in Figure 4. Then label the following on Earth at an equinox AND a solstice position.

    North Pole and South Pole
    Axis of Earth
    Equator, Tropic of Cancer, Tropic of Capricorn
    Arctic Circle and Antarctic Circle
    Circle of illumination (day–night line)

Questions 14–19 refer to the June **solstice** position of Earth in Figure 4.

14. What term is used to describe the June 21–22 date in each hemisphere?

    Northern Hemisphere: _____ solstice

    Southern Hemisphere: _____ solstice

15. On June 21–22 the Sun's rays are perpendicular to Earth's surface at noon at the (Tropic of Cancer, equator, Tropic of Capricorn). Circle your answer.

16. What latitude is receiving the most intense solar energy on June 21–22?

    Latitude: _____

17. Toward what direction, north or south, would you look to see the Sun at noon on June 21–22 if you lived at the following latitudes?

    40°N latitude: _____

    10°N latitude: _____

18. Position a rubber band, string, or pieces of tape on a globe corresponding to the *circle of illumination* on June 21–22. Then determine the approximate length of daylight at the following latitudes by examining the proportionate number of degrees of longitude a place located at each latitude spends in daylight as Earth rotates. (*Note:* Earth rotates a total of 360° of longitude per day. Therefore, each 15° of longitude is equivalent to one hour.)

    70°N latitude: _____ hrs _____ min

    40°S latitude: _____ hrs _____ min

    40°N latitude: _____ hrs _____ min

    90°S latitude: _____ hrs _____ min

     0° latitude: _____ hrs _____ min

19. On June 21–22, latitudes north of the Arctic Circle are receiving (6, 12, 24) hours of daylight, while latitudes south of the Antarctic Circle are experiencing (6, 12, 24) hours of darkness. Circle your answers.

Questions 20–24 refer to the December solstice position of Earth in Figure 4.

20. What name is used to describe the December 21–22 date in each hemisphere?

    Northern Hemisphere: _____ solstice

    Southern Hemisphere: _____ solstice

21. On December 21–22 the Sun's rays are perpendicular to Earth's surface at noon on the (Tropic of

Table 1   Length of Daylight

LATITUDE (DEGREES)	SUMMER SOLSTICE	WINTER SOLSTICE	EQUINOXES
0	12 h	12 h	12 h
10	12 h 35 min	11 h 25 min	12
20	13 12	10 48	12
30	13 56	10 04	12
40	14 52	9 08	12
50	16 18	7 42	12
60	18 27	5 33	12
66.5	24 h	0 00	12
70	24 h (for 2 mo)	0 00	12
80	24 h (for 4 mo)	0 00	12
90	24 h (for 6 mo)	0 00	12

Cancer, equator, Tropic of Capricorn). Circle your answer.

22. On December 21–22 the (Northern, Southern) Hemisphere is receiving the most intense solar energy. Circle your answer.

23. If you lived at the equator, on December 21–22 you would look (north, south) to see the Sun at noon.

24. Refer to Table 1, "Length of daylight." What is the length of daylight at each of the following latitudes on December 21–22?

   90°N latitude: _____ hrs _____ min

   40°S latitude: _____ hrs _____ min

   40°N latitude: _____ hrs _____ min

   90°S latitude: _____ hrs _____ min

   0° latitude: _____ hrs _____ min

Questions 25–31 refer to the March and September **equinox** positions of Earth in Figure 4.

25. For those living in the Northern Hemisphere, what terms are used to describe the following dates?

   March 21: _____ equinox

   September 22: _____ equinox

26. For those living in the Southern Hemisphere, what terms are used to describe the following dates?

   March 21: _____ equinox

   September 22: _____ equinox

27. On March 21 and September 22 the Sun's rays are perpendicular to Earth's surface at noon at the (Tropic of Cancer, equator, Tropic of Capricorn). Circle your answer.

28. What latitude is receiving the most intense solar energy on March 21 and September 22?

   Latitude: _____

29. If you lived at 20°S latitude, you would look (north, south) to see the Sun at noon on March 21 and September 22. Circle your answer.

30. What is the relation between the North and South Poles and the circle of illumination on March 21 and September 22?

   _____

31. Write a brief statement describing the length of daylight everywhere on Earth on March 21 and September 22.

   As you have seen, the latitude where the noon Sun is directly overhead (vertical, or 90° above the horizon) is easily determined for the solstices and equinoxes.

   Figure 5 is a graph, called an **analemma**, that can be used to determine the latitude where the overhead noon Sun is located for any date. To determine the lat-

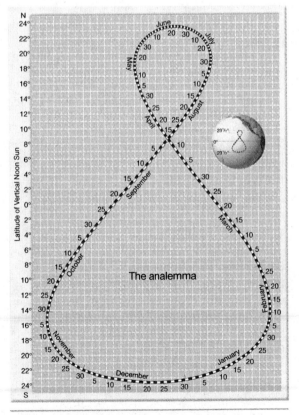

Figure 5   The analemma, a graph illustrating the latitude of the overhead (vertical) noon Sun throughout the year.

itude of the overhead noon Sun from the analemma, find the desired date on the graph and read the coinciding latitude along the left axis. Don't forget to indicate North or South when writing latitude.

32. Using a colored pencil, draw lines on Figure 5 that correspond to the equator, Tropic of Cancer, and Tropic of Capricorn. Label each of these special parallels of latitude on the figure.

33. Using the analemma, Figure 5, determine where the Sun is overhead at noon on the following dates.

    December 10: _____

    March 21:   _____

    May 5:   _____

    June 22:   _____

    August 10:   _____

    October 15:   _____

34. The position of the overhead noon Sun is always located on or between which two parallels of latitude?

    _____°N (named the Tropic of _____) and

    _____°S (named the Tropic of _____)

35. The overhead noon Sun is located at the equator on September _____ and March _____. Together, these two days are called the _____. Fill in your answers.

36. Refer to Figure 5 and write a brief paragraph summarizing the yearly movement of the overhead noon Sun and how the intensity and duration of solar radiation varies over Earth's surface throughout the year.

    _____

    _____

    _____

Calculating Noon Sun Angle

Knowing where the noon Sun is overhead on any given date (the analemma), you can determine the angle above the horizon of the noon Sun at any other latitude on that same day. The relation between latitude and **noon Sun angle** is

> For each degree of latitude that the place is away from the latitude where the noon Sun is overhead, the angle of the noon Sun becomes one degree *lower* from being vertical (or 90°) above the horizon (Figure 6).

37. Complete Table 2 by calculating the noon Sun angle for each of the indicated latitudes on the

Table 2   Noon Sun Angle Calculations

LATITUDE OF OVERHEAD NOON SUN	MAR 21 ( )	APR 11 ( )	JUN 21 ( )	DEC 22 ( )
		Noon Sun Angle		
90°N	___	___	___	___
40°N	50°	___	___	26½°
0°	___	___	66½°	___
20°S	___	62°	___	___

dates given. Some of the calculations have already been done.

38. From Table 2, the highest average noon Sun angle occurs at (40°N, 0°, 20°S). Circle your answer.

39. Calculate the noon Sun angle for your latitude on today's date.

    Date: _____

    Latitude of overhead noon Sun: _____

    Your latitude: _____

    Your noon Sun angle: _____

    (*Note:* You may want to compare your calculated noon Sun angle with a measured noon Sun angle obtained by using the technique described in the exercise "Astronomical Observations.")

40. Calculate the maximum and minimum noon Sun angles for your latitude.

MAXIMUM NOON SUN ANGLE	MINIMUM NOON SUN ANGLE
Date: _____	Date: _____
Angle: _____°	Angle: _____°

41. Calculate the average noon Sun angle (maximum plus minimum, divided by 2) and the range of the noon Sun angle (maximum minus minimum) for your location.

    Average noon Sun angle = _____°

    Range of the noon Sun angle = _____°

42. Describe some situations in which knowing the noon Sun angle might be useful.

    _____

    _____

Using Noon Sun Angle

One very practical use of noon Sun angle is in navigation. Like a navigator, you can determine your latitude if the date and angle of the noon Sun at your location are known. As you answer questions 43 and 44, keep in mind the relation between latitude and noon Sun angle (Figure 6).

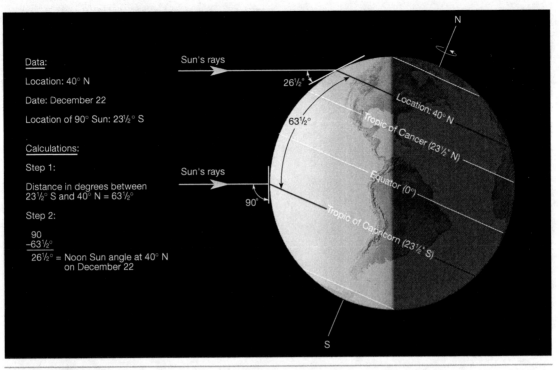

Figure 6 Calculating the noon Sun angle. Recall that on any given day, only one latitude receives vertical (90°) rays of the Sun. A place located 1° away (either north or south) receives an 89° angle at any location; a place 2° away, an 88° angle, and so forth. To calculate the noon Sun angle, simply find the number of degrees of latitude separating that location from the latitude that is receiving the vertical rays of the Sun. Then subtract that value from 90°. The example in this figure illustrates how to calculate the noon Sun angle for a city located at 40° north latitude on December 22 (winter solstice).

43. What is your latitude if, on March 21, you observe the noon Sun to the north at 18° above the horizon?

    Latitude: _____

44. What is your latitude if, on October 16, you observe the noon Sun to the south at 39° above the horizon?

    Latitude: _____

Solar Radiation at the Outer Edge of the Atmosphere

Table 3 shows the average daily radiation received at the outer edge of the atmosphere at select latitudes for different months.

To help visualize the pattern, plot the data from Table 3 on the graph in Figure 7. Using a different color for each latitude, draw lines through the monthly values to obtain yearly curves. Then answer questions 45–48.

45. Why do two periods of maximum solar radiation occur at the equator?

    _____

46. In June, why does the outer edge of the atmosphere at the equator receive less solar radiation than both the North Pole and 40°N latitude?

    _____

    _____

47. Why does the outer edge of the atmosphere at the North Pole receive no solar radiation in December?

    _____

48. What would be the approximate monthly values for solar radiation at the outer edge of the atmosphere at 40°S latitude? Explain how you arrived at the values.

    March: _____

    June: _____

    September: _____

    December: _____

    Explanation: _____

    _____

Table 3 Solar Radiation at the Outer Edge of the Atmosphere (langleys/day) at Various Latitudes during Select Months

LATITUDE	MARCH	JUNE	SEPTEMBER	DECEMBER
90°N	50	1050	50	0
40°N	700	950	720	325
0°	890	780	880	840

Earth–Sun Relations on the Internet

Apply the concepts from this exercise to an examination of solar and terrestrial radiation by completing the corresponding online activity on the *Applications & Investigations in Earth Science* website at http://prenhall.com/earthsciencelab

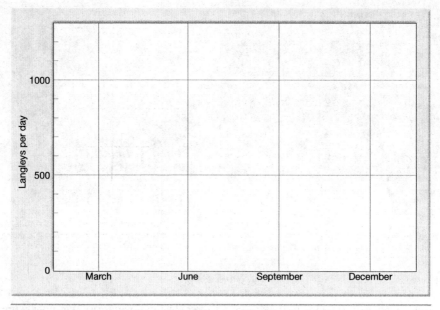

Figure 7 Graph of solar radiation received at the outer edge of the atmosphere.

Earth–Sun Relations

Date Due: _____

Name: _____

Date: _____

Class: _____

After you have finished this exercise, complete the following questions. You may have to refer to the exercise for assistance or to locate specific answers. Be prepared to submit this summary/report to your instructor at the designated time.

1. From Figure 3, what was the calculated percentage of solar radiation that is intercepted by each of the following 30° segments of latitude?

   0°–30° _____ %

   30°–60° _____ %

   60°–90° _____ %

2. How many hours of daylight occur at the following locations on the specified dates?

	MARCH 22	DECEMBER 22
40°N	_____ hrs	_____ hrs
0°	_____ hrs	_____ hrs
90°S	_____ hrs	_____ hrs

3. What is the noon Sun angle at these latitudes on April 11?

   40°N _____ °   0° _____ °

4. What is the relation between the angle of the noon Sun and the quantity of solar radiation received per square centimeter at the outer edge of the atmosphere?

   _____

   _____

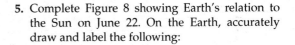

Figure 8 Earth's relation to the Sun on June 22.

5. Complete Figure 8 showing Earth's relation to the Sun on June 22. On the Earth, accurately draw and label the following:

   Axis
   Equator
   Tropic of Cancer
   Tropic of Capricorn
   Antarctic Circle
   Arctic Circle
   Circle of illumination
   Location of the overhead noon Sun

6. What causes the intensity and duration of solar radiation received at any place to vary throughout the year?

   _____

   _____

   _____

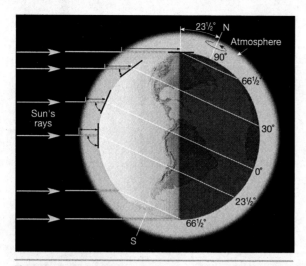

Figure 9   Earth–Sun relation diagram.

7. What is the date illustrated by the diagram in Figure 9? Calculate the noon Sun angle at 30° N latitude on this date and write a paragraph describing the distribution of solar radiation over Earth on this date.

   _____

   _____

   _____

   _____

8. What are the maximum and minimum noon Sun angles at your latitude?

   Maximum noon Sun angle =   _____° on _____ (date)

   Minimum noon Sun angle =   _____° on _____ (date)

9. What are the maximum and minimum durations of daylight at your latitude?

   Maximum duration of daylight =   _____ hrs

   Minimum duration of daylight =   _____ hrs

10. Write a brief statement describing how the intensity and duration of solar radiation change at your location throughout the year.

    _____

    _____

    _____

    _____

    _____

11. The day is March 22. You view the noon Sun to the south at 35° above the horizon. What is your latitude?

    Latitude: _____

4

Name: _____   **Laboratory Section:** _____

Date: _____   **Score/Grade:** _____

Lab Exercise

Contours and Topographic Maps

An important diagnostic tool for landform analysis is the **topographic map.** While specific application and analysis of topographic maps relating to various types of landforms will be dealt with in later exercises, some concepts used to interpret topographic maps have applications in other kinds of maps that will be used in discussing weather topics. **Isolines**, lines connecting points of equal value, are seen on topographic maps as **contour lines,** lines connecting points of equal elevation. Other isolines such as isotherms (equal temperatures), isobars (equal atmospheric pressure), and isohyets (equal precipitation) will be used in analyzing weather patterns. Therefore, a familiarity with reading and interpreting isolines will be useful at this point. A general discussion of topographic maps and contour lines is the focus of this lab. It features five sections and two optional Google Earth™ mapping service questions. These optional questions allow you to compare the topographic maps and your work in the lab manual with Google Earth™ mapping service imagery and topographic maps draped over the landscape.

Key Terms and Concepts

Alber's projection
contour interval
contour lines
geographic index number
index contours
isogonic chart
local relief
map view
planimetric map

profile view
relief
stereoscopic contour map
topography
topographic map
Universal Transverse Mercator (UTM) grid
vertical datum
vertical exaggeration

Objectives

After completion of this lab, you should be able to:

1. *Construct* contour lines (isolines of equal elevation) and *interpret* a mapped landscape.
2. *Construct* a topographic profile and *calculate* an appropriate vertical exaggeration for a profile.
3. *Describe* and *use* the legend and marginal labels and information on a topographic quadrangle map.

Materials/Sources Needed

pencils
color pencils
calculator
compass
protractor
ruler
stereoscope

Lab Exercise and Activities

✳ SECTION 1

Contour Lines and Topographic Maps

The USGS depicts information on *quadrangle maps*, rectangular maps bounded by parallels and meridians rather than by political boundaries. A conic map projection, the **Alber's projection** (equal-area), is used as a base for these quadrangle maps (see outside of fold-out flap on back cover). Two standard parallels (where the cone intersects the globe's surface) are used to improve the accuracy in conformality and scale for the conterminous United States: 29.5° N and 45.5° N latitudes (Figure 1). For the U.S. Mapping Program the standard parallels are shifted for conic projection base maps of Alaska (55° N and 65° N) and Hawai'i (8° N and 18° N).

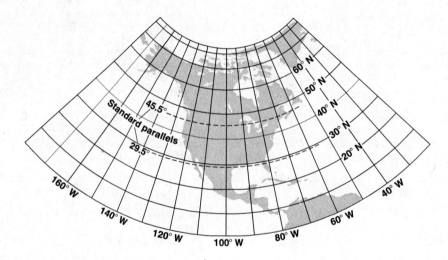

Figure 1
Alber's equal-area conic projection, standard parallels of 29.5° N and 45.5° N; a standard for the U.S. National Mapping Program.

In mapping, a basic **planimetric map** is first prepared, showing the horizontal position of boundaries; land-use aspects; and political, economic, and social features. A highway map, such as one that you may have in your car, is a common example of a planimetric map. A vertical scale of physical features is then added to portray the terrain. The most popular and widely used of these maps are the detailed **topographic maps** prepared by the USGS.

Topographic maps portray physical **relief**, the change in elevation between the highest point and lowest point on the map. (*Local relief* refers to the change in elevation between two specified points on the map.) Relief is indicated through the use of elevation **contour lines**. A contour line connects all points at the same elevation above or below a stated reference level. This reference level—usually mean sea level—is called the *vertical datum*. The *contour interval* is the difference in elevation between two adjacent contour lines. (In Figure 2 the contour interval is 20 ft or 6.1 m; in Figure 4 the contour interval is 40 ft or 12.2 m.)

More specifics on contour lines:

a) Contour lines are typically printed in *brown color* on topographic maps.

b) All points along a contour line are at the same elevation—a contour line is an *isoline* depicting equal elevation.

c) Contour lines separate areas of higher (upslope) elevation from areas of lower (downslope) elevation.

d) Given a large enough map, contour lines always form a closed polygon although on a smaller map contour lines may run off the margin.

e) The *contour interval* is the difference in elevation between two adjacent contour lines.

f) Contour lines only touch where there is a steep cliff and never cross unless the cliff face has an overhanging ledge (hidden contours are then depicted as dashed lines).

g) Contour lines spaced closer together depict a steeper slope; whereas a wider spacing of contour lines depict a gentler slope.

h) Concentric, closed contours denote a hill or summit; whereas a similar pattern with *hachure marks* (small tick marks) on the downslope side depicts a closed depression.

i) When the map is showing a depression, the first hachured contour line is the same elevation as the adjacent lower contour line.

j) Contour lines form an upstream-pointing, V-shaped pattern wherever contour lines cross a stream.

k) Contour lines occur in pairs from one side of a valley to the other side.

l) Index contours are thicker and usually have their elevation labelled.

The topographic map in Figure 2 shows a hypothetical landscape that demonstrates how contour lines and intervals depict slope and relief. Slope is indicated by the pattern of lines and the space between them. The steeper a slope or cliff, the closer together the contour lines appear in Figure 2b; note the narrowly spaced contours representing the cliff. A more gradual slope is portrayed by a wider spacing of these contour lines, as you can see from the widely spaced lines on the beach.

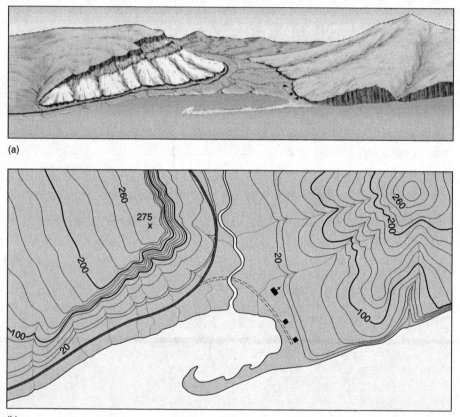

(a)

(b)

Figure 2
Perspective view of a hypothetical landscape (a); topographic map of that landscape (b). (After the U.S. Geological Survey.)

Use the hypothetical landscape and topographic map in Figure 2 to answer the following questions:

1. What is the contour interval? _____

   How can you tell?
   _____

2. In terms of local relief (the difference between the highest and the lowest elevation): what is the relief on the

   west (left) side of the highway? _____ on the east (right) side of the highway? _____

3. What is the highest point on the map and what is its elevation? _____

4. Imagine that you are planning a *low-exertion* walk from the church, across the river to the high point on the west side of this landscape. First on Figure 2a and then on Figure 2b use a red color pencil to draw the route you would take; give your reasons for choosing this easier route in terms of elevation change per distance traveled.

   _____

   _____

   _____

5. On each figure use a blue pencil to draw in streams, using arrows to show the direction of stream flow. Note there is a main stream in the valley and at least four tributary streams or creeks. How do the contour lines indicate the direction of flow?

   _____

   _____

   _____

Contour lines and contour maps are two-dimensional images portraying relief, which is a three-dimensional concept. A **stereoscopic contour map** (also called a *stereogram*) helps to see these contour lines in three dimensions. Figure 3 shows two views of a hill and valley area: (a) is a contour map, and (b) is a stereoscopic contour map.

    Use the stereolenses provided with your manual to view Figure 3b in three dimensions and compare this view with features marked on the contour map Figure 3a.

A. Each contour line connects points of equal elevation.
B. Varying degrees of steepness are obvious: the steepest areas where the lines are closest together.
C. Widely spaced contours depict where the slope is gentle.
D. Contour lines crossing stream valleys form a V pointing upstream.
E. Hills are indicated by a series of closed, concentric contours.
F. Depression contours have hachure marks on the downslope side. The hachures are not marked on the stereo pairs in Figure 3b as are on the contour map in Figure 3a, but the depression is clearly evident as you view the stereo pair in 3-D through the stereoscope.

Once you become adept at reading contour lines, you will be able to "see" the relief, even though the maps are only in two dimensions. Stereograms will be used again in later lab activities when we examine landforms.

(a)   CONTOUR INTERVAL 20 FEET

(b)

Figure 3
Contour map (a) and stereoscopic contour map (b) of the same hill and valley landscape. (From Horace MacMahan, Jr., *Stereogram Book of Contours*. Copyright © 1995, by Hubbard Scientific Company, pp. 8-9. Reprinted by permission of American Educational Products, Hubbard Scientific.)

❋ SECTION 2

Constructing Contour Lines

Figure 4 presents elevation values for a selected landscape. The contour interval is 40 feet, and *index contours* (thicker lines—on this map every fifth contour, marked with the line's elevation) at 200 feet, 400 feet, and 600 feet are drawn for you in bold isolines. A river channel is noted on the map flowing along a valley separated from the ocean by a ridge. The elevation of the channel is marked at three locations.

Use Figure 4 to do the following work and answer the questions.

1. Using a pencil, sketch 40-foot-interval contour lines using the specific site elevations given. Note that we have drawn the 40-ft contour line for you. You must *interpolate* (estimate) elevations between known values. Draw your contour lines lightly at first as you determine the best portrayal, then darken in your work and erase stray pencil marks. (Do not worry if your lines go through the elevation labels.) Remember the contour line basics given in ❋ SECTION 1.
    The coastline is the datum—mean sea level. *Begin your work at the coast and work inland.* (Hint: make this task easier by color-coding the elevations in 40-foot intervals. Circle all elevations from 0-40 feet in green, 41-80 feet in yellow, etc. Then, when drawing the contour lines, you will be "grouping" the colors, with the contour lines as separators between the color groups.)

2. Three vertical control bench marks, indicated by the letters "BM" and marked with an "x," are noted on the map. What are their elevations?

    _____

3. Three other specific spot elevations are noted with an "x." What are their elevations?

    _____

4. What effect do the intermittent (periodically dry) stream channels have on the topography of the region?

    _____

5. Given the trend and location of the 40-foot elevation contour, if you were walking along the water's edge, how would you characterize the topography and relief of the coastline? Steep? Gentle relief?

    _____

6. In what compass direction does the river flow? How can you tell? (See ❋ SECTION 1, question 5.)

    _____

7. Which portion of the map has the greatest relief? _____

8. **Challenge question:** If you were assigned the task of building a single general aviation runway of 3700 feet in length, where would you place it? Draw your runway plan on the map to the correct scale. (Make it 100 feet wide.) Give your reasons for this site selection.

    _____

    _____

9. Google Earth™ mapping service optional question. Stewart's Point Quadrangle. For the KMZ file and questions go to http://prenhall.com/christopherson/lm

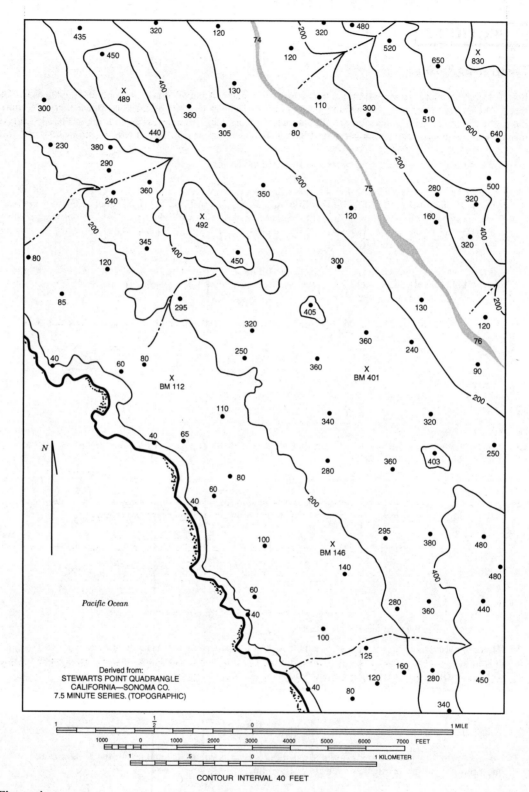

Figure 4
A portion of the Stewarts Point quadrangle, enlarged and adapted with 200-, 400-, and 600-foot index contours highlighted.

✳ SECTION 3

Topographic Profile

Relief refers to vertical elevation differences in a local landscape. The character and general configuration of Earth's surface is called **topography**, the feature portrayed so effectively on topographic maps. In Figure 4 of this exercise you constructed contour lines and completed an analysis of a coastal landscape. The local topography included a coastal marine platform (terrace), low ridge, stream valley, and hill. The maximum relief on the map was approximately 700 feet, averaging about 400 feet.

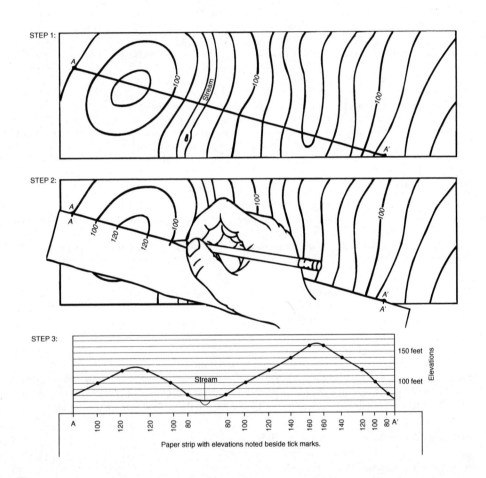

Figure 5
Constructing a topographic profile using the edge of a piece of paper. (From Busch, Richard M., editor, *Laboratory Manual in Physical Geology*, 3 ed., Macmillan Publishing Company © 1993.)

An important method of topographic map analysis is construction of a **topographic profile**, the graphic representation of graduated elevations along a line segment drawn on a map. A *map view*, or *plan view*, is the normal way we view a map as if we were looking straight down from above ("bird's-eye" view). A cross section of a landscape—as if you sliced through the strata and obtained a side view—is a *profile view* and is demonstrated in Figure 5. The profile view shows you the "shape" of the land and demonstrates a line-of-sight perspective. As you work with topographic profiles, allow yourself to develop methods with which you are comfortable.

One method of preparing a profile is to draw a line connecting two points (a *transect*) along which you want to obtain the profile (Figure 5, Step 1). Take a piece of paper, fold the paper over and crease it for a stiff straight edge. The paper can be plain or graph paper. Lay the folded edge along the drawn line. Make tick marks at each point where a contour line makes contact with the edge of the paper and note the elevation at that point. These will represent elevation points on the profile graph (Step 2). Carry the tick marks down to the graph at the appropriate elevation, plotting each point; connect the points with a smooth curved line to complete the profile (Step 3).

Construct your first topographic profile using Figure 6. Portrayed is an enlarged portion of the Palmyra, New York, quadrangle. The western New York region was blanketed by various advances and retreats of continental glaciers. The geomorphic feature you are profiling was deposited by a glacier.

A prepared graph is supplied with the figure; however, let's briefly discuss how it is set up. Note in Figure 6 that the horizontal scale of the map is 1:12,000, or 1″ = 1000′ If we used this same scale for the vertical axis on the topographic profile graph, the local relief of 192 feet would only cover 0.192 inch on the graph. To construct a readable and useful profile a technique of **vertical exaggeration** is employed. In this figure a vertical scale of 1:1200, or 1′ = 100′ is used and represents a 10 × (times) exaggeration of the horizontal scale. Other landscapes require different vertical exaggerations—*the greater the maximum relief of a landscape the greater the scale should be* to conveniently fit on a graph for analysis. For instance, the greater relief in Figure 7 made an exaggeration of 3.3 × (times) more appropriate as compared to the 10 × exaggeration in Figure 6. The horizontal scale should be left at the same scale as the map.

Follow the procedure illustrated in Figure 5 to construct a profile along the line drawn in Figure 6, making tick marks at each point where the drawn line and contour lines intersect. Carry the elevations denoted by the tick marks down to the graph, plotting each point. The steeper the slope the closer the points are placed; a gentle slope places them farther apart. The last step is to connect the points with a smooth curved line to visualize the relief and topography of this landscape. You may want to shade the area below the line to better display the profile.

Use the profile constructed in Figure 6 to answer the following:

1. What distance does this topographic profile cover?_____

2. What is the maximum relief along this profile?_____

3. The landform feature you have profiled is a drumlin. Drumlins are formed by glacial deposits and are streamlined in the direction of the glacier's movement. They have a blunt end upstream, a tapered end downstream, and a rounded summit. Using your protractor, what direction was the glacier flowing?

   _____

4. Using the 500-foot contour, what is the width of this feature?_____

5. If we used a vertical scale identical to the horizontal scale, how many squares on the graph would

   accommodate the maximum relief along the profile?_____

6. Google Earth™ mapping service optional question. Palmyra quadrangle drumlin. For the KMZ file and questions go to http://prenhall.com/christopherson/lm

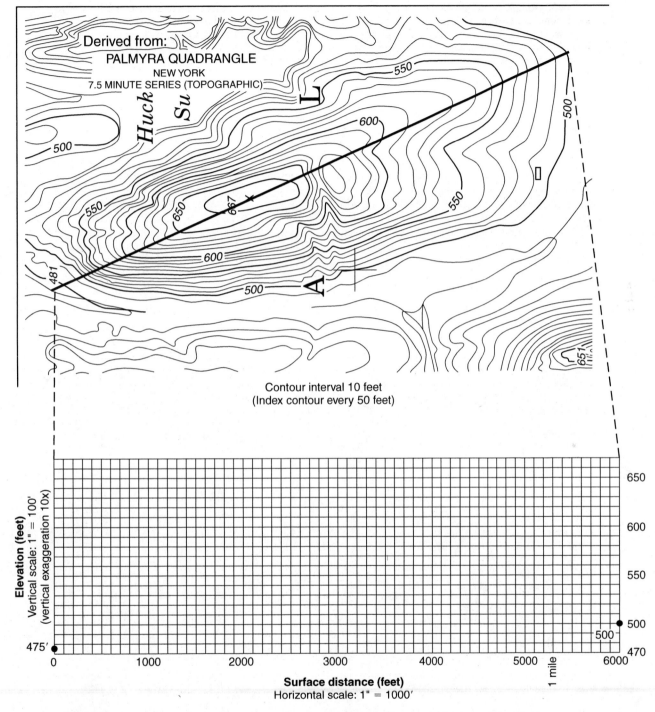

Figure 6
Topographic profile from a portion of the Palmyra, New York quadrangle (enlarged).

A second example of a vertical profile is in Figure 7. Using the same procedure as you did on the previous assignment, construct a topographic profile. Label the South Fork of the Gualala River (see Figure 5, Step 3), the bench mark at 112 feet, and various road crossings on your profile. The coastline forms a contour line of equal elevation—sea level. Note the change in contour interval and scale from that of Figure 6.

Use Figure 7 to answer further questions about preparing a topographic profile.

7. What is the length of this topographic profile in miles? . . . in kilometers? _____

8. How wide is the marine terrace (a relatively flat platform or "shelf" along the coast) in miles?

    _____ . . . in kilometers? _____

9. If we used a vertical scale identical to the horizontal scale, how many squares on the graph would

    accommodate the maximum relief along the profile? _____

10. What is the relief (elevation difference between the highest and lowest points, in a local landscape) in the

    river valley along southwest slopes? _____

    . . . along the northeast slopes? _____

11. Can you physically see the shoreline when standing at the summit at 731 feet elevation? Explain.

    _____

    _____

    Can you see the marine terrace from the summit? _____

    Can you see the northwest end of the runway at Sea Ranch Airport (a point just south of the profile) from the

    summit? _____ Explain. _____

    _____

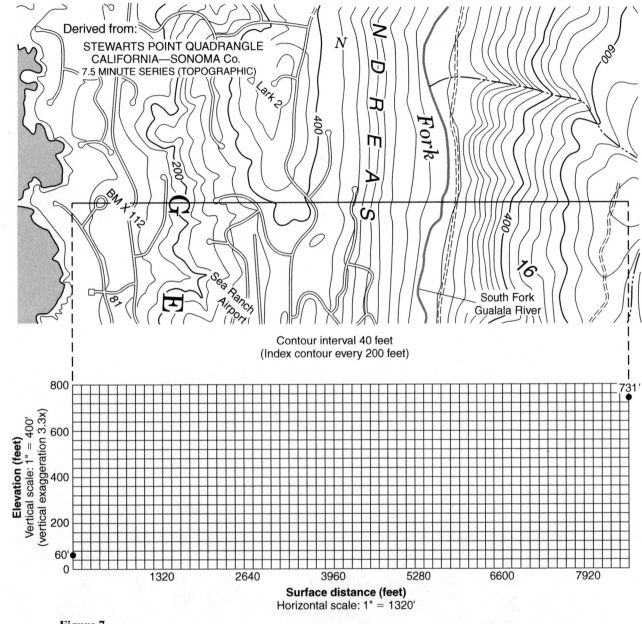

Figure 7
Topographic profile from a portion of the Stewarts Point, California quadrangle map (enlarged). From west to east along the profile, this landscape features a coastal marine terrace, a ridge, a river valley, and a hill rising to 731 feet above sea level. The coastline forms a contour line of equal elevation.

✴ SECTION 4

Interpreting Topographic Map Information

Topographic maps in the series of quadrangle maps prepared by the USGS, or Centre for Topographic Information in Canada, provide a wealth of information. Have your lab instructor show you an index map for your state or province that portrays all the quadrangle map coverage available. Your lab instructor will provide you with a topographic map sheet to examine as you follow along with this description of its elements.

The name of the topographic map quadrangle is given in the upper-right corner, with the state name, and 15-minute or 7.5-minute series designation; if it is a 7.5-minute quad. This also signifies which portion of the published 15-minute quad it represents ("SW/4, NE/4," etc.). Other grids, in addition to latitude/longitude, are in use, so geographic coordinates of both State Plane and the Universal Transverse Mercator (UTM) grid systems are listed near the corner margins of the quad map. The Public Lands Survey township and range system is also noted.

COUNCIL BLUFFS NORTH QUADRANGLE
IOWA–NEBRASKA
7.5 MINUTE SERIES (TOPOGRAPHIC)

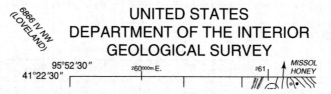

The lower-right corner carries the name of the quad; portion of 15-minute quad, if applicable; geographic index number; and the year of the map. The *geographic index number* is derived from the latitude and longitude of the lower-right corner of the map. Each corner also features complete geographic coordinates.

COUNCIL BLUFFS NORTH, IOWA—NEBR.
N4115–W9545/7.5

1956

PHOTOREVISED 1969 AND 1975

AMS 6866 IV SE—SERIES V876

The upper-left corner always carries the same credit line for the primary government agent for U.S. mapping.

UNITED STATES
DEPARTMENT OF THE INTERIOR
GEOLOGICAL SURVEY

A more complete credit line and map preparation history is in the lower-left margin. If cooperative assistance from another entity was only minor, this may be listed in this place. A variety of such information might be featured in this label.

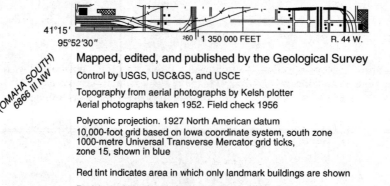

Mapped, edited, and published by the Geological Survey

Control by USGS, USC&GS, and USCE

Topography from aerial photographs by Kelsh plotter
Aerial photographs taken 1952. Field check 1956

Polyconic projection. 1927 North American datum
10,000-foot grid based on Iowa coordinate system, south zone
1000-metre Universal Transverse Mercator grid ticks,
zone 15, shown in blue

Red tint indicates area in which only landmark buildings are shown

Revisions shown in purple compiled from aerial photographs
taken 1969 and 1975. This information not field checked

Purple tint indicates extension of urban areas

Where applicable note the names of adjoining topographic quadrangles at each corner and along the sides. If this reference appears, you can assume that the map name refers to a quad at the same scale and the same series.

38°37'30"
123°22'30"

Earth's geographic North Pole and magnetic North Pole locations do not coincide. In addition the magnetic pole slowly migrates from year to year. The lower left-center margin features a magnetic declination diagram for the year of the map field survey or date of map revision. This declination is taken from an *isogonic map* that maps magnetic declination. This diagram allows you to correct compass bearing readings when using the topographic map. A state map graphically shows the location of the quad in the lower right-center margin. Here are some samples of this designation.

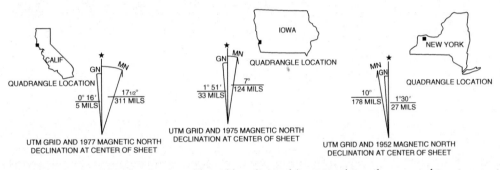

The map scale (representative fraction and graphic or bar scale), contour intervals, any supplementary contour intervals, vertical datum ("National Geodetic Vertical Datum of 1929" appears on post-1975 maps), depth or sounding information in bodies of water, and sales information are shown in the lower-center margin of the map sheet.

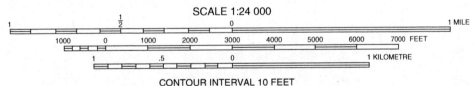

SCALE 1:24 000

CONTOUR INTERVAL 10 FEET
NATIONAL GEODETIC VERTICAL DATUM OF 1929

A complete map symbol key should be used for interpreting the map (inside front cover of this lab manual), although road symbols used for the quad are shown in the lower-right corner.

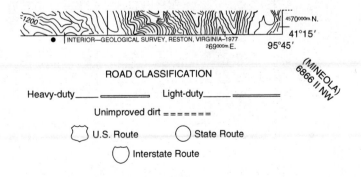

INTERIOR—GEOLOGICAL SURVEY, RESTON, VIRGINIA—1977

4570000m. N.
41°15'
269000m. E.   95°45'

(MINEOLA)
6866 II NW

ROAD CLASSIFICATION

Heavy-duty _____   Light-duty _____
Unimproved dirt = = = = = = =
⬡ U.S. Route   ◯ State Route
⬇ Interstate Route

Use a topographic map *provided by your lab instructor* to answer the following:

1. Name, state, and series of the map:_____

   _____

2. If a 7.5-minute map, give its location and position relative to the 15-minute series quad for this region:

   _____

3. Did any other agencies or entities participate in the preparation of this map?

   _____

4. List the geographic index number for this quad:

   _____

5. Denote the latitude and longitude of each corner of the quad map:

   N. E. corner: _____

   S. E. corner: _____

   S. W. corner: _____

   N. W. corner: _____

6. List the nearest UTM (Universal Transverse Mercator) coordinate for the upper right corner of the map:

   _____

7. Describe the complete map history and credit line:

   _____

   _____

   _____

8. If you needed to obtain the maps adjoining this quadrangle, what are their names? Label these names along the appropriate sides and corners on the quadrangle.

9. What is the representative fraction scale for this map?_____

Convert this to a written (verbal) scale. (Show your work)

_____

10. Using the graphic or bar scale on the map, determine the distance in kilometers between two points selected

by your instructor. The points are: _____ and _____.

Distance in kilometers _____; and, miles _____.

11. Calculate the total area of the map in square kilometers. (Show your work.)_____

And, in square miles. (Show your
work.)_____

12. What is the magnetic declination for your quadrangle map? _____

Which direction (and how many degrees) would you have to turn in order to adjust for this declination?

_____

To what azimuth would your compass needle point? _____

Hikers and backpackers frequently include topographic maps and compasses among their equipment.
Magnetic declination must be taken into account when using a compass, and adjustments must be made. To
do this, simply superimpose the magnetic compass points (based on the declination arrow) over the true north
compass points (N, E, W, S). It is easy to see that, if the magnetic declination is 10°E, you must turn 10°
west, so that your compass north arrow is pointing to 350° ($360° − 10° = 350°$).

13. List any additional information provided in the margins of this particular map quadrangle:

_____

_____

_____

Your instructor may want to provide you with additional questions pertaining to the topographic map that has
been selected for this activity. Questions may include features specific to the chosen map and use of symbols
for which you might need to consult the topographic map legend on the inside front cover of this manual.

✳ SECTION 5

Topographic Map Sources

1. List at least 3 sources where you might purchase topographic maps; include both local and distant sources (mail order).

    a) _____

    b) _____

    c) _____

2. Prior to this class, have you ever used topographic maps? _____

    If yes, explain. _____

    _____

3. Other than in this class, when might you use topographic maps?

    _____

    _____

5

Atmospheric Heating

The quantity of radiation from the Sun that strikes the outer edge of Earth's atmosphere at any one place is not constant but varies with the seasons. This exercise examines, step by step, what happens to **solar radiation** as it passes through the atmosphere, is absorbed at Earth's surface, and is reradiated by land and water back to the atmosphere (Figure 1). Investigating the journey of solar radiation and how it is influenced and modified by air, land, and water will provide a better understanding of one of the most basic weather elements, atmospheric temperature.

Objectives

After you have completed this exercise, you should be able to:

1. Explain how Earth's atmosphere is heated.
2. Describe the effect that the atmosphere has on absorbing, scattering, and reflecting incoming solar radiation.
3. List the gases in the atmosphere that are responsible for absorbing long-wave radiation.
4. Explain how the heating of a surface is related to its albedo.
5. Discuss the differences in the heating and cooling of land and water.
6. Summarize the global pattern of surface temperatures for January and July.
7. Describe how the temperature of the atmosphere changes with increasing altitude.
8. List the cause of a surface temperature inversion.
9. Determine the effect that wind speed has on the windchill equivalent temperature.

Materials

calculator
colored pencils

Figure 1 Solar radiation and atmospheric heating. (Photo by E. J. Tarbuck)

Materials Supplied by Your Instructor

light source
black and silver
  containers
two thermometers

wood splints
beaker of sand
beaker of water

Terms

solar radiation
greenhouse
  effect
terrestrial
  radiation

albedo
environmental
  lapse rate
temperature
  inversion

isotherm
windchill
  equivalent
  temperature

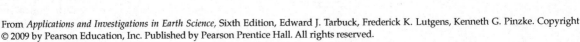

Introduction

Temperature is an important element of weather and climate because it greatly influences air pressure, wind, and the amount of moisture in the air. The unequal heating that takes place over the surface of Earth is what sets the atmosphere in motion, and the movement of air is what brings changes in our weather.

The single greatest cause for temperature variations over the surface of Earth is differences in the reception of solar radiation. Secondary factors such as the differential heating of land and water, ocean currents, and altitude can modify local temperatures.

The amount of solar energy (radiation) striking Earth is not constant throughout the year at any particular place, nor is it uniform over the face of Earth at any one time. However, the total amount of radiation that the planet intercepts from the Sun equals the total radiation that it loses back to space. It is this balance between incoming and outgoing radiation that keeps Earth from becoming continuously hotter or colder.

Solar Radiation at the Outer Edge of the Atmosphere

The two factors that control the amount of solar radiation that a square meter receives at the outer edge of the atmosphere, and eventually Earth's surface, are the Sun's *intensity* and its *duration*. You may want to review the exercise "Earth-Sun Relations."

1. Briefly define solar intensity and duration.

   Intensity of solar radiation: _____

   _____

   Duration of solar radiation: _____

   _____

2. Complete Table 1 by calculating the angle that the noon Sun would strike the outer edge of the atmosphere at each of the indicated latitudes on the specified date. How many hours of daylight would each place experience on these dates?

Table 1   Noon Sun Angle and Length of Day

	March 21		June 21	
	NOON SUN ANGLE	LENGTH OF DAY	NOON SUN ANGLE	LENGTH OF DAY
40°N:	____°	____ hrs	____°	____ hrs
0°:	____°	____ hrs	____°	____ hrs
40°S:	____°	____ hrs	____°	____ hrs

3. Explain the reason why the intensity and duration of solar radiation received at the outer edge of the atmosphere is not constant at any particular latitude throughout the year.

_____

_____

Atmospheric Heating

Atmospheric heating is a function of (1) the ability of atmospheric gases to absorb radiation, (2) the amount of solar radiation that reaches Earth's surface, and (3) the nature of the surface material. Of the three, selective absorption of radiation by the atmosphere provides an insight into the mechanism of atmospheric heating. The quantity of radiation that reaches Earth's surface and the ability of the surface to absorb and reradiate the radiation determine the extent of atmospheric heating.

The atmosphere is rather selective and efficiently absorbs long-wave radiation that we detect as heat while allowing the transmission of most of the short wavelengths—a process called the **greenhouse effect**. The short-wave radiation that reaches Earth's surface and is absorbed ultimately returns to the atmosphere in the form of long-wave, **terrestrial radiation**. As the radiation travels up from the surface through the atmosphere, it is absorbed by atmospheric gases, heating the atmosphere from below. Since terrestrial radiation supplies most of the long-wave radiation to the atmosphere, it is the primary source of heat. The fact that temperature typically decreases with an increase in altitude in the lower atmosphere is clear evidence supporting this mechanism of atmospheric heating.

Solar Radiation Received at Earth's Surface

As solar radiation travels through the atmosphere, it may be reflected, scattered, or absorbed. The effect of the atmosphere on incoming solar radiation and the amount of radiation that ultimately reaches the surface is primarily dependent upon the angle at which the solar beam passes through the atmosphere and strikes Earth's surface.

Figure 2 illustrates the atmospheric effects on incoming solar radiation for an average noon Sun angle. Answer questions 4–7 by examining the figure and supplying the correct response.

4. _____ % of the incoming solar radiation is reflected and scattered back to space.

5. _____ % of the incoming solar radiation is absorbed by gases in the atmosphere and clouds.

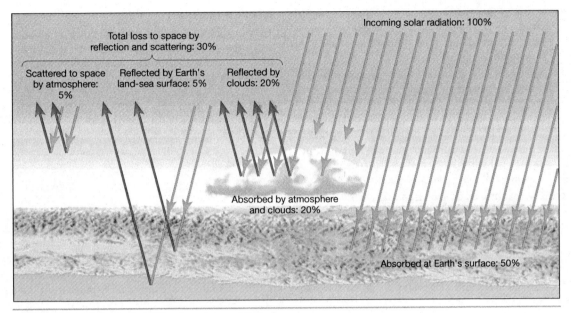

Figure 2   Solar radiation budget of the atmosphere and Earth.

6. _____ % of the incoming solar radiation is absorbed at Earth's surface.

7. (Two and a half, Four) times as much incoming radiation is absorbed by Earth's surface than by the atmosphere and clouds. Circle your answer.

Figure 3 illustrates the effects of the atmosphere on various wavelengths of radiation. Use Figure 3 to answer questions 8–11 by circling the correct response.

8. The incoming solar radiation that passes through the atmosphere and is absorbed at Earth's surface is primarily in the form of (ultraviolet, visible, infrared) wavelengths.

9. When the surface releases the solar radiation it has absorbed, this terrestrial radiation is primarily (ultraviolet, visible, infrared) wavelengths.

10. (Ultraviolet, Visible, Infrared) wavelengths of radiation are absorbed efficiently by oxygen and ozone in the atmosphere.

11. Oxygen and ozone are (good, poor) absorbers of infrared radiation.

12. (Nitrogen, Carbon dioxide) and (water vapor, ozone) are the two principal gases that absorb most of the terrestrial radiation in the atmosphere.

Assume Figure 2 represents the atmospheric effects on incoming solar radiation for an average noon Sun angle of about 50°. Answer questions 13–16 concerning other noon Sun angles by circling the appropriate responses.

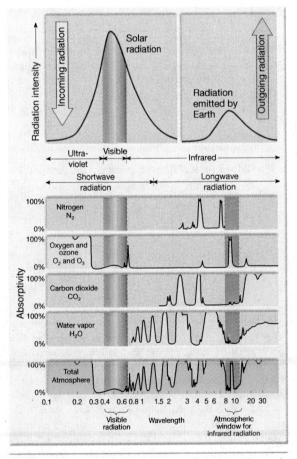

Figure 3   The absorptivity of selected gases of the atmosphere and the atmosphere as a whole.

13. If the noon Sun angle is 90°, solar radiation would have to penetrate a (greater, lesser) thickness of atmosphere than with an average noon Sun angle.

14. The result of a 90° noon Sun angle would be that (more, less) incoming radiation would be reflected, scattered, and absorbed by the atmosphere and (more, less) radiation would be absorbed and reradiated by Earth's surface to heat the atmosphere.

15. If the noon Sun angle is 20°, solar radiation would have to penetrate a (greater, lesser) thickness of atmosphere than with an average noon Sun angle.

16. The result of a 20° noon Sun angle would be that (more, less) incoming radiation would be reflected, scattered, and absorbed by the atmosphere and (more, less) radiation would be absorbed and reradiated by Earth's surface to heat the atmosphere.

17. How is the angle (intensity) at which the solar beam strikes Earth's surface related to the quantity of solar radiation received by each square meter?

_____

_____

18. How is the length of daylight related to the quantity of solar radiation received by each square meter at the surface?

_____

_____

_____

19. Write a brief statement summarizing the mechanism responsible for heating the atmosphere.

_____

_____

_____

The Nature of Earth's Surface

The various materials that comprise Earth's surface play an important role in determining atmospheric heating. Two significant factors are the **albedo** of the surface and the different abilities of land and water to absorb and reradiate radiation.

Albedo is the reflectivity of a substance, usually expressed as the percentage of radiation that is reflected from the surface. Since surfaces with high albedos are not efficient absorbers of radiation, they cannot return much long-wave radiation to the atmosphere for heating.

Albedo Experiment

To better understand the effect of color on albedo, observe the equipment in the laboratory (Figure 4) and then conduct the following experiment by completing each of the indicated steps.

Step 1: Write a brief hypothesis stating the heating and cooling of light-versus dark-colored surfaces.

_____

_____

_____

Step 2: Place the black and silver containers (with lids and thermometers) about six inches away from the light source. Make certain that both containers are of equal distance from the light and are not touching one another.

Step 3: Record the starting temperature of both containers on the albedo experiment data table, Table 2.

Step 4: Turn on the light and record the temperature of both containers on the data table at about 30-second intervals for 5 minutes.

Step 5: Turn off the light and continue to record the temperatures at 30-second intervals for another 5 minutes.

Step 6: Plot the temperatures from the data table on the albedo experiment graph, Figure 5. Use a different color line to connect the points for each container.

Figure 4 Albedo experiment lab equipment.

Table 2   Albedo Experiment Data Table

	STARTING TEMPERATURE	30 SEC	1 MIN	1.5 MIN	2 MIN	2.5 MIN	3 MIN	3.5 MIN	4 MIN	4.5 MIN	5 MIN	5.5 MIN	6 MIN	6.5 MIN	7 MIN	7.5 MIN	8 MIN	8.5 MIN	9 MIN	9.5 MIN	10 MIN
Black container																					
Silver container																						

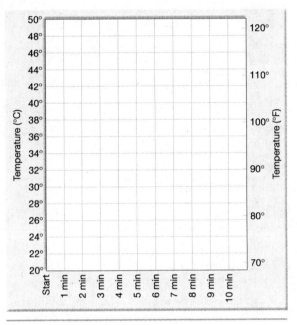

Figure 5   Albedo experiment graph.

20. For each container, calculate the *rate of heating* (change in temperature divided by the time the light was on) and the *rate of cooling* (change in temperature divided by the time the light was off).

	Heating Rate	Cooling Rate
Silver can:	_____	_____
Black can:	_____	_____

21. Write a statement that summarizes and explains the results of your albedo experiment.

_____

_____

_____

_____

22. What are some Earth surfaces that have high albedos and some that have low albedos?

High albedos: _____

Low albedos: _____

23. Given equal amounts of radiation reaching the surface, the air over a snow-covered surface will be (warmer, colder) than air above a dark-colored, barren field. Circle your answer. Then explain your choice fully in terms of what you have learned about albedo.

_____

_____

24. If you lived in an area with long, cold winters, a (light-, dark-) colored roof would be the best choice for your house. Circle your answer. Explain the reasons for your choice.

_____

_____

Land and Water Heating Experiment

Land and water influence the air temperatures above them in different manners because they do not absorb and reradiate energy equally.

Investigate the differential heating of land and water by observing the equipment in the laboratory (Figure 6) and conducting the following experiment by completing each of the indicated steps.

Step 1: Fill one beaker three-quarters full with dry sand and a second beaker three-quarters full with water at room temperature.

Step 2: Using a wood splint, suspend a thermometer in each beaker so that the bulbs are *just below* the surfaces of the sand and water.

Step 3: Hang a light from a stand so it is equally as close as possible to the top of the two beakers.

Step 4: Record the starting temperatures for both the dry sand and water on the land and water heating data table, Table 3.

Figure 6   Land and water heating experiment lab equipment.

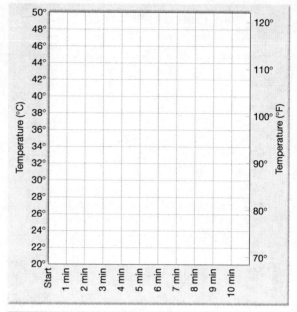

Figure 7   Land and water heating graph.

ferent color line to connect the points for each material.

25. Questions 25a and 25b refer to the land and water heating experiment.

    a. How do the abilities to change temperature differ for dry sand and water when they are exposed to equal quantities of radiation?

    _____

    _____

    b. How do the abilities to change temperature differ for dry sand and damp sand when they are exposed to equal quantities of radiation?

    _____

    _____

Step 5: Turn on the light and record the temperature on the data table at about one-minute intervals for 10 minutes.

Step 6: Turn off the light for several minutes. Dampen the sand with water and record the starting temperature of the damp sand on the data table. Turn on the light and record the temperature of the damp sand on the data table at about one-minute intervals for 10 minutes.

Step 7: Plot the temperatures for the water, dry sand, and damp sand from the data table on the land and water heating graph, Figure 7. Use a dif-

Table 3	Land and Water Heating Data Table										
	STARTING TEMPERATURE	1 MIN	2 MIN	3 MIN	4 MIN	5 MIN	6 MIN	7 MIN	8 MIN	9 MIN	10 MIN
Water											
Dry sand											
Damp sand											

26. Suggest several reasons for the differential heating of land and water.

_____

_____

_____

_____

Figure 8 presents the annual temperature curves for two cities, A and B, that are located in North America at approximately 37°N latitude. On any date both cities receive the same intensity and duration of solar radiation. One city is in the center of the continent, while the other is on the west coast. Use Figure 8 to answer questions 27–34.

27. In Figure 8, city (A, B) has the highest mean monthly temperature. Circle your answer.

28. City (A, B) has the lowest mean monthly temperature.

29. The greatest *annual temperature range* (difference between highest and lowest mean monthly temperatures) occurs at city (A, B).

30. City (A, B) reaches its maximum mean monthly temperature at an earlier date.

31. City (A, B) maintains a more uniform temperature throughout the year.

32. Of the two cities, city A is most likely located (along a coast, in the center of a continent).

33. The most likely location for city B is (coastal, mid-continent).

34. Describe the effect that the location, along the coast or in the center of a continent, has on the temperature of a city.

_____

_____

Atmospheric Temperatures

Air temperatures are not constant. They normally change (1) through time at any one location, (2) with latitude because of the changing sun angle and length of daylight, and (3) with increasing altitude in the lower atmosphere because the atmosphere is primarily heated from the bottom up.

Daily Temperatures

In general, the daily temperatures that occur at any particular place are the result of long-wave radiation being released at Earth's surface. However, secondary factors, such as cloud cover and cold air moving into the area, can also cause significant variations.

Questions 35–42 refer to the daily temperature graph, Figure 9.

35. The coolest temperature of the day occurs at _____. Fill in your answer.

36. The warmest temperature occurs at _____.

37. What is the *daily temperature range* (difference between maximum and minimum temperatures for the day)?

Daily temperature range: _____ °F (_____ °C).

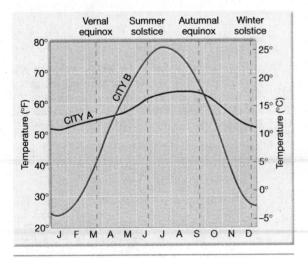

Figure 8 Mean monthly temperatures for two North American cities located at approximately 37°N latitude.

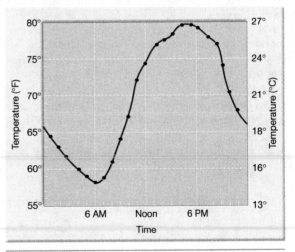

Figure 9 Typical daily temperature graph for a mid-latitude city during the summer.

38. What is the *daily temperature mean* (average of the maximum and minimum temperatures)?

    Daily temperature mean: _____ °F (_____ °C).

39. Refer to the mechanism for heating the atmosphere. Why does the warmest daily temperature occur in mid-to-late afternoon rather than at the time of the highest Sun angle?

    _____

    _____

40. Why does the coolest temperature of the day occur about sunrise?

    _____

    _____

41. How would cloud cover influence daily maximum and minimum temperatures?

    _____

    _____

42. On Figure 9 sketch and label a colored line that best represents a daily temperature graph for a typical cloudy day.

Global Pattern of Temperature

The primary reason for global variations in surface temperatures is the unequal distribution of radiation over the Earth. Among the most important secondary factors are differential heating of land and water, ocean currents, and differences in altitude.

Questions 43–55 refer to Figure 10, "World Distribution of Mean Surface Temperatures (°C) for January and July." The lines on the maps, called **isotherms**, connect places of equal surface temperature.

43. The general trend of the isotherms on the maps is (north–south, east–west). Circle your answer.

44. In general, how do surface temperatures vary from the equator toward the poles? Why does this variation occur?

    _____

    _____

    _____

45. The warmest and coldest temperatures occur over which countries or oceans?

    Warmest global temperature: _____

    _____

    Coldest global temperature: _____

    _____

46. The locations of the warmest and coldest temperatures are over (land, water).

47. Calculate the *annual temperature range* at each of the following locations:

    Coastal Norway at 60°N: _____ °C (_____ °F)

    Siberia at 60°N, 120°E: _____ °C (_____ °F)

    On the equator over the center of the Atlantic Ocean: _____ °C (_____ °F)

48. Explain the large annual range of temperature in Siberia.

    _____

    _____

49. Why is the annual temperature range smaller along the coast of Norway than at the same latitude in Siberia?

    _____

    _____

50. Why is temperature relatively uniform throughout the year in the tropics?

    _____

    _____

51. Using the two maps in Figure 10, calculate the approximate average annual temperature range for your location. How does your temperature range compare with those in the tropics and Siberia?

    Average annual temperature range:

    _____ °C (_____ °F)

    _____

    _____

52. Trace the path of the 5°C isotherm over North America in January. Explain why the isotherm de-

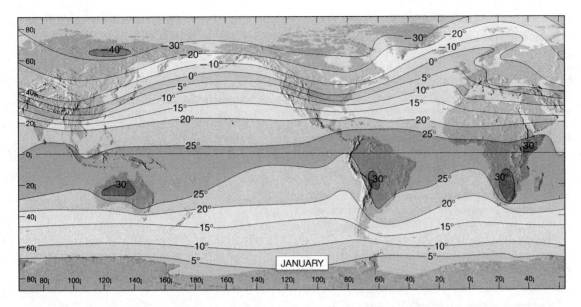

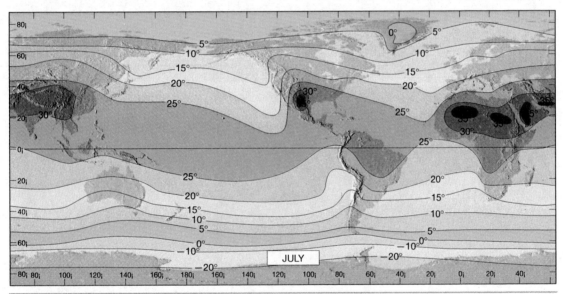

Figure 10   World distribution of mean surface temperatures (°C) for January and July.

viates from a true east–west trend where it crosses from the Pacific Ocean onto the continent.

_____

_____

53. Trace the path of the 20°C isotherm over North America in July. Explain why the isotherm deviates from a true east–west trend where it crosses from the Pacific Ocean onto the continent.

_____

_____

54. Why do the isotherms in the Southern Hemisphere follow a true east–west trend more closely than those in the Northern Hemisphere?

_____

_____

55. Why does the entire pattern of isotherms shift northward from the January map to the July map?

_____

_____

Temperature Changes with Altitude

Since the primary source of heat for the lower atmosphere is Earth's surface, the normal situation found in the lower 12 kilometers of the atmosphere is a decrease in temperature with increasing altitude. This temperature decrease with altitude in the lower atmosphere is called the **environmental lapse rate**. However, at altitudes from about 12 to 45 kilometers, the atmospheric absorption of incoming solar radiation causes temperature to increase.

Use Figure 11 to answer questions 56–60.

56. Using the temperature curve as a guide, label the *troposphere, mesosphere, stratosphere,* and *thermosphere* on the atmospheric temperature curve, Figure 11.

57. On Figure 11, mark with a line and label the *tropopause, mesopause,* and *stratopause.*

58. What is the approximate temperature of the atmosphere at each of the following altitudes?

    10 km: _____ °C (_____ °F)

    50 km: _____ °C (_____ °F)

    80 km: _____ °C (_____ °F)

59. Using Figure 11, calculate the average decrease in temperature with altitude of the troposphere in both °C/km and °F/mi.

    _____

60. Explain the reason for each of the following:

    Temperature decrease with altitude in the troposphere:

    _____

    _____

    Temperature increase in the stratosphere:

    _____

    _____

    Temperature increase in the thermosphere:

    _____

    _____

Figure 11   Atmospheric temperature curve.

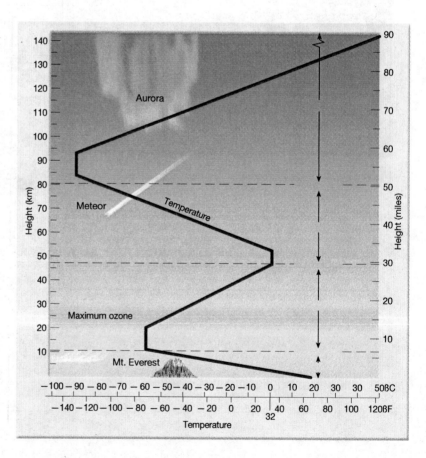

61. Of what importance is the gas *ozone* in the stratosphere? What will be the effect on radiation received at Earth's surface of a decrease of ozone in the stratosphere?

_____

_____

_____

Assume the average, or normal, environmental lapse rate (temperature decrease with altitude) in the troposphere is 3.5°F per 1,000 feet (6.5°C per kilometer).

62. If the surface temperature is 60°F (16°C), what would be the approximate temperature at 20,000 feet (6,000 meters)?

_____ °F (_____ °C)

63. If the surface temperature is 80°F (27°C), at approximately what altitude would a pilot expect to find each of the following atmospheric temperatures?

50°F: _____ feet (10°C: _____ meters)

0°C: _____ meters (32°F: _____ feet)

Periodically, the temperature near the surface of Earth increases with altitude. This situation, which is opposite from the normal condition, is called a **temperature inversion**.

64. Suggest a possible cause for a surface temperature inversion.

_____

_____

Windchill Equivalent Temperature

Windchill equivalent temperature is the term applied to the sensation of temperature that the human body feels, in contrast to the actual temperature of the air as recorded by a thermometer. Wind cools by evaporating perspiration and carrying heat away from the body. When temperatures are cool and the wind speed increases, the body reacts as if it were being subjected to increasingly lower temperatures—a phenomenon known as *windchill*.

65. Refer to the windchill equivalent temperature chart, Figure 12. What is the windchill equivalent temperature sensed by the human body in the following situations?

Air Temperature (°F)	Wind Speed (mph)	Windchill Equivalent Temperature (°F)
30°	10	_____
−5°	20	_____
−20°	30	_____

66. Write a brief summary of the effect of wind speed on how long a person can be exposed before frostbite develops.

_____

_____

_____

Atmospheric Heating on the Internet

Research current and historical atmospheric temperatures at your location by completing the corresponding online activity on the *Applications & Investigations in Earth Science* website at http://prenhall.com/ earth-sciencelab

Temperature (°F)																		
Calm	40	35	30	25	20	15	10	5	0	−5	−10	−15	−20	−25	−30	−35	−40	−45
5	36	31	25	19	13	7	1	−5	−11	−16	−22	−28	−34	−40	−46	−52	−57	−63
10	34	27	21	15	9	3	−4	−10	−16	−22	−28	−35	−41	−47	−53	−59	−66	−72
15	32	25	19	13	6	0	−7	−13	−19	−26	−32	−39	−45	−51	−58	−64	−71	−77
20	30	24	17	11	4	−2	−9	−15	−22	−29	−35	−42	−48	−55	−61	−68	−74	−81
25	29	23	16	9	3	−4	−11	−17	−24	−31	−37	−44	−51	−58	−64	−71	−78	−84
30	28	22	15	8	1	−5	−12	−19	−26	−33	−39	−46	−53	−60	−67	−73	−80	−87
35	28	21	14	7	0	−7	−14	−21	−27	−34	−41	−48	−55	−62	−69	−76	−82	−89
40	27	20	13	6	−1	−8	−15	−22	−29	−36	−43	−50	−57	−64	−71	−78	−84	−91
45	26	19	12	5	−2	−9	−16	−23	−30	−37	−44	−51	−58	−65	−72	−79	−86	−93
50	26	19	12	4	−3	−10	−17	−24	−31	−38	−45	−52	−60	−67	−74	−81	−88	−95
55	25	18	11	4	−3	−11	−18	−25	−32	−39	−46	−54	−61	−68	−75	−82	−89	−97
60	25	17	10	3	−4	−11	−19	−26	−33	−40	−48	−55	−62	−69	−76	−84	−91	−98

Wind (mph)

Frostbite Times   ☐ 30 minutes   ☐ 10 minutes   ☐ 5 minutes

Figure 12 This windchill chart came into use in November 2001. Fahrenheit temperatures are used here because this is how the National Weather Service and the news media in the United States commonly report windchill information. The shaded areas on the chart indicate frostbite danger. Each shaded zone shows how long a person can be exposed before frostbite develops. (*After NOAA, National Weather Service*)

Notes and calculations.

Atmospheric Heating

Date Due: _____

Name: _____

Date: _____

Class: _____

After you have finished this exercise, complete the following questions. You may have to refer to the exercise for assistance or to locate specific answers. Be prepared to submit this summary/report to your instructor at the designated time.

1. Assume an average noon Sun angle. What percentage of the solar radiation will be absorbed by the atmosphere and what percentage will be absorbed by Earth's surface?

   Atmospheric absorption: _____ %

   Absorption by Earth's surface: _____ %

2. What will be the atmospheric effect of each of the following?

   Less ozone in the stratosphere:

   _____

   _____

   More carbon dioxide in the atmosphere:

   _____

   _____

   A surface with a high albedo:

   _____

   _____

3. Briefly explain how Earth's atmosphere is heated.

   _____

   _____

   _____

4. What are the primary heat-absorbing gases in the atmosphere? In general, what wavelength of radiation do they absorb?

   _____

   _____

5. What were the starting and 5-minute temperatures you obtained for the black and silver containers in the albedo experiment?

	STARTING TEMPERATURE	5-MINUTE TEMPERATURE
Black container:	_____	_____
Silver container:	_____	_____

6. Summarize the effect of color on the heating of an object.

   _____

   _____

7. What were the starting and ending temperatures you obtained for the water and dry sand in the land and water heating experiment?

	STARTING TEMPERATURE	ENDING TEMPERATURE
Water:	_____	_____
Dry sand:	_____	_____

67

8. Summarize the effects that equal amounts of radiation have on the heating of land and water.

_____

_____

9. Where are the highest and lowest average monthly temperatures located on Earth?

Highest average monthly temperature:

_____

_____

Lowest average monthly temperature:

_____

_____

10. Why does the Northern Hemisphere experience a greater annual range of temperature than the Southern Hemisphere?

_____

_____

11. Define each of the following:

Environmental lapse rate:

_____

_____

Windchill equivalent temperature:

_____

_____

Troposphere:

_____

_____

12. Referring to the average temperature graphs for Spokane and Seattle, Washington, shown in Figure 13, discuss the reason(s) why the two graphs are dissimilar, even though both cities are at about the same latitude.

_____

_____

_____

_____

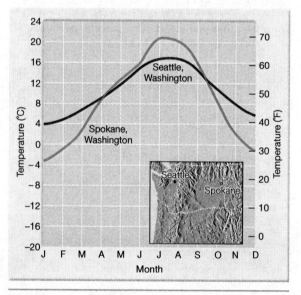

Figure 13 Temperature graphs for Spokane and Seattle, WA.

6

Atmospheric Moisture, Pressure, and Wind

By observing, recording, and analyzing weather conditions, meteorologists attempt to define the principles that control the complex interactions that occur in the atmosphere (Figure 1). No analysis of the atmosphere is complete without an investigation of the remaining variables—humidity, precipitation, pressure, and wind.

This exercise examines the changes of state of water, how the water vapor content of the air is measured, and the sequence of events necessary to cause cloud formation. Global patterns of precipitation, pressure, and wind are also reviewed. Although the elements are presented separately, keep in mind that all are very much interrelated. A change in any one element often brings about changes in the others.

Objectives

After you have completed this exercise, you should be able to:

1. Explain the processes involved when water changes state.
2. Use a psychrometer or hygrometer and appropriate tables to determine the relative humidity and dew-point temperature of air.
3. Explain the adiabatic process and its effect on cooling and warming the air.
4. Calculate the temperature and relative humidity changes that take place in air as the result of adiabatic cooling.
5. Describe the relation between pressure and wind.
6. Describe the global patterns of surface pressure and wind.

Materials

calculator   ruler   colored pencils

Figure 1   Developing storm clouds. (Photo by E. J. Tarbuck)

Materials Supplied by Your Instructor

psychrometer or hygrometer   hot plate
beaker, ice, thermometer   thumbtacks
barometer   cardboard
atlas   tape

Terms

water vapor	relative humidity	psychrometer/
evaporation	saturated	hygrometer
precipitation	dew-point	condensation
latent heat	temperature	nuclei
dry adiabatic rate	equatorial low	Coriolis effect
wet adiabatic rate	subtropical high	trade winds
atmospheric	subpolar low	westerlies
pressure	anticyclone	polar easterlies
barometer	cyclone	monsoon
isobar	wind	

Atmospheric Moisture and Precipitation

Water vapor, an odorless, colorless gas produced by the **evaporation** of water, comprises only a small percentage of the lower atmosphere. However, it is an important atmospheric gas because it is the source of all **precipitation**, aids in the heating of the atmosphere by absorbing radiation, and is the source of **latent heat** (hidden or stored heat).

Changes of State

The temperatures and pressures that occur at and near Earth's surface allow water to change readily from one state of matter to another. The fact that water can exist as a gas, liquid, or solid within the atmosphere makes it one of the most unique substances on Earth. Use Figure 2 to answer questions 1–4.

1. To help visualize the processes and heat requirements for changing the state of matter of water, write the name of the process involved (choose from the list) and whether heat is absorbed or released by the process at the indicated locations by each arrow in Figure 2.

PROCESSES

Freezing	Evaporation	Deposition
Sublimation	Melting	Condensation

2. To melt ice, heat energy must be (absorbed, released) by the water molecules. Circle your answer.

3. The process of condensation requires that water molecules (absorb, release) heat energy. Circle your answer.

4. The energy requirement for the process of deposition is the (same as, less than) the total energy required to condense water vapor and then freeze the water. Circle your answer.

Latent Heat Experiment

This experiment will help you gain a better understanding of the role of heat in changing the state of matter. You are going to heat a beaker that contains a mixture of ice and water (Figure 3). You will record temperature changes *as the ice melts* and continue to record the temperature changes *after the ice melts*. Conduct the experiment by completing the following steps.

Step 1: Write a brief hypothesis as to how you expect the temperature of the ice-water mixture to change as heat energy is added.

_____

_____

_____

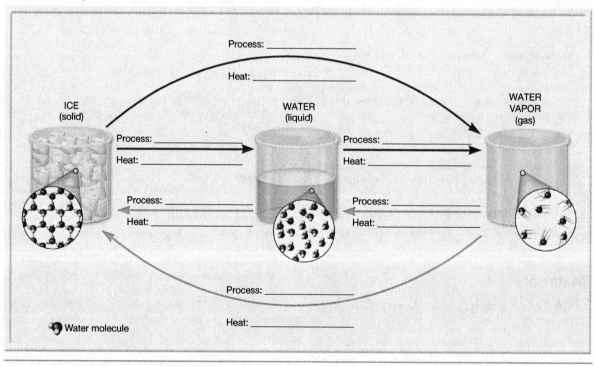

Figure 2   Changes of state of water.

Thermometer →

Figure 3 Latent heat experiment equipment.

Table 1   Latent Heat Data Table

TIME (MINUTES)	TEMPERATURE (° ____)
Starting	_____
1	_____
2	_____
3	_____
4	_____
5	_____
6	_____
7	_____
8	_____
9	_____
10	_____
11	_____
12	_____
13	_____
14	_____
15	_____

Questions 5–8 refer to your latent heat experiment.

5. How did the temperature of the mixture change prior to, and after, the ice had melted?

_____

_____

6. Calculate the average temperature change per minute of the ice-water mixture prior to the ice

Step 2: Turn on the hot plate and set the temperature setting to about three-fourths maximum (7 on a scale of 10).

CAUTION: The hot plate will become hot quickly. Do not touch the heating surface.

Step 3: Fill a 400-ml or larger beaker approximately half full with ice and add enough COLD water to cover the ice.

Step 4: Gently stir the ice-water mixture about 15 seconds with the thermometer and record the temperature in the "Starting" temperature space on the data table, Table 1.

Step 5: Place the beaker with the ice-water mixture and thermometer on the hot plate, and while STIRRING THE MIXTURE CONSTANTLY, record the temperature of the mixture at *one-minute intervals* on the data table. Watch the ice closely as it melts. *Note the exact time on the data table when all the ice has melted.*

Step 6: Continue stirring the mixture and recording its temperature for at least 3 or 4 minutes after all the ice has melted.

Step 7: Plot the temperatures from the data table on the graph, Figure 4.

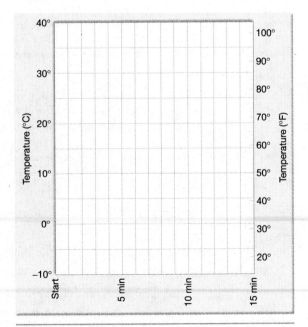

Figure 4 Latent heat experiment graph.

melting and the average rate after the ice had melted.

Average rate prior to melting: _____

Average rate after melting: _____

7. With your answers to questions 5 and 6 in mind, write a statement comparing your results to your hypothesis in **Step 1**.

_____

_____

8. With reference to the absorption or release of latent (hidden) heat, explain why the temperature changed at a different rate after the ice melted as compared to before all the ice had melted.

_____

_____

_____

Water-Vapor Capacity of Air

Any measure of water vapor in the air is referred to as *humidity*. The amount of water vapor required for saturation is directly related to temperature.

The mass of water vapor in a unit of air compared to the remaining mass of dry air is referred to as the *mixing ratio*. Table 2 presents the mixing ratios of saturated air (water vapor needed for saturation) at various temperatures. Use the table to answer questions 9–12.

9. To illustrate the relation between the amount of water vapor needed for saturation and temperature, prepare a graph by plotting the data from Table 2 on Figure 5.

10. From Table 2 and/or Figure 5, what is the water vapor content at saturation of a kilogram of air at each of the following temperatures?

    40°C: _____ grams/kilogram

    68°F: _____ grams/kilogram

    0°C: _____ grams/kilogram

    −20°C: _____ grams/kilogram

11. From Table 2, raising the air temperature of a kilogram of air 5°C, from 10°C to 15°C, (increases, decreases) the amount of water vapor needed

Table 2   Amount of Water Vapor Needed to Saturate a Kilogram of Air at Various Temperatures, the Saturation Mixing Ratio

TEMPERATURE		WATER VAPOR CONTENT AT SATURATION (g/kg)
(°C)	(°F)	
−40	−40	0.1
−30	−22	0.3
−20	−4	0.75
−10	14	2
0	32	3.5
5	41	5
10	50	7
15	59	10
20	68	14
25	77	20
30	86	26.5
35	95	35
40	104	47

for saturation by (3, 6) grams. However, raising the temperature from 35°C to 40°C (increases, decreases) the amount by (8, 12) grams. Circle your answers.

12. Using Table 2 and/or Figure 5, write a statement that relates the amount of water vapor needed for saturation to temperature.

_____

_____

_____

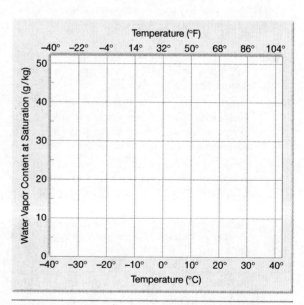

Figure 5 Graph of water vapor content at saturation of a kilogram of air versus temperature.

Measuring Humidity

Relative humidity is the most common measurement used to describe water vapor in the air. In general, it expresses how close the air is to reaching saturation at that temperature. Relative humidity is a *ratio* of the air's actual water vapor *content* (amount actually in the air) compared with the amount of water vapor required for saturation at that temperature (saturation mixing ratio), expressed as a percent. The general formula is

$$\text{Relative humidity (\%)} = \frac{\text{Water vapor content}}{\text{Saturation mixing ratio}} \times 100$$

For example, from Table 2, the saturation mixing ratio of a kilogram of air at 25°C would be 20 grams per kilogram. If the actual amount of water vapor in the air was 5 grams per kilogram (the water vapor content), the relative humidity of the air would be calculated as follows:

$$\text{Relative humidity (\%)} = \frac{5\,\text{g/kg}}{20\,\text{g/kg}} \times 100 = 25\%$$

13. Use Table 2 and the formula for relative humidity to determine the relative humidity for each of the following situations of identical temperature.

AIR TEMPERATURE	WATER VAPOR CONTENT	RELATIVE HUMIDITY
15°C	2 g/kg	____%
15°C	5 g/kg	____%
15°C	7 g/kg	____%

14. From question 13, if the temperature remains constant, adding water vapor will (raise, lower) the relative humidity, while removing water vapor will (raise, lower) the relative humidity. Circle your answers.

15. Use Table 2 and the formula for relative humidity to determine the relative humidity for each of the following situations of identical water vapor content.

AIR TEMPERATURE	WATER VAPOR CONTENT	RELATIVE HUMIDITY
25°C	5 g/kg	____%
15°C	5 g/kg	____%
5°C	5 g/kg	____%

16. From question 15, if the amount of water vapor in the air remains constant, cooling will (raise, lower) the relative humidity, while warming will (raise, lower) the relative humidity. Circle your answers.

17. In the winter, air is heated in homes. What effect does heating have on the relative humidity inside the home? What can be done to lessen this effect?

_____

_____

18. Explain why the air in a cool basement is humid (damp) in the summer.

_____

_____

19. Write brief statements describing each of the two ways that the relative humidity of air can be changed.

1. _____

2. _____

One of the misconceptions concerning relative humidity is that it alone gives an accurate indication of the actual quantity of water vapor in the air. For example, on a winter day if you hear on the radio that the relative humidity is 90%, can you conclude that the air contains more water vapor than on a summer day that records a 40% relative humidity? Completing question 20 will help you find the answer.

20. Use Table 2 to determine the water vapor content for each of the following situations. As you do the calculations, keep in mind the definition of relative humidity.

SUMMER	WINTER
Air temperature = 77°F	Air temperature = 41°F
Relative humidity = 40%	Relative humidity = 90%
Content = _____ g/kg	Content = _____ g/kg

21. Explain why relative humidity does *not* give an accurate indication of the actual amount of water vapor in the air.

_____

_____

_____

Dew-Point Temperature

Air is **saturated** when it contains all the water vapor that it can hold at a particular temperature. The temperature at which saturation occurs is called the **dew-point temperature**. Put another way, the dew point is the temperature at which the relative humidity of the air is 100%.

Previously, in question 15, you determined that a kilogram of air at 25°C, containing 5 grams of water vapor had a relative humidity of 25% and was not saturated. However, when the temperature was lowered to 5°C, the air had a relative humidity of 100% and was saturated. Therefore, 5°C is the dewpoint temperature of the air in that example.

22. By referring to Table 2, what is the dew-point temperature of a kilogram of air that contains 7 grams of water vapor?

    Dew-point temperature = _____°C

23. What is the relative humidity and dew-point temperature of a kilogram of 25°C air that contains 10 grams of water vapor?

    Relative humidity = _____%

    Dew-point temperature = _____°C

Using a Psychrometer or Hygrometer

The relative humidity and dew-point temperature of air can be determined by using a **psychrometer** (Figure 6) or **hygrometer** and appropriate charts. The psychrometer consists of two thermometers mounted side by side. One of the thermometers, the *dry-bulb* thermometer, measures the air temperature. The other thermometer, the *wet-bulb thermometer,* has a piece of wet cloth wrapped around its bulb. As the psychrometer is spun for approximately one minute, water on the wet-bulb thermometer evaporates and cooling results. In dry air, the rate of evaporation will be high, and a low wet-bulb temperature will be recorded. After using the instrument and recording both the dry- and wet-bulb temperatures, the relative humidity and dew-point temperature are determined using Table 3, "Relative Humidity (percent)" and Table 4, "Dew-Point Temperature." With a hygrometer, relative humidity can be read directly, without the use of tables.

24. Use Table 3 to determine the relative humidity for each of the following psychrometer readings.

	READING 1	READING 2
Dry-bulb temperature:	20°C	32°C
Wet-bulb temperature:	18°C	25°C
Difference between dry- and wet-bulb temperatures:	____	____
Relative humidity:	____%	____%

Figure 6 Sling psychrometer. The sling psychrometer is one instrument that is used to determine relative humidity and dew-point temperature. (Photo by E. J. Tarbuck)

25. From question 24, what is the relation between the *difference* in the dry-bulb and wet-bulb temperatures and the relative humidity of the air?

    _____

    _____

26. Use Table 4 to determine the dew-point temperature for each of the following two psychrometer readings.

	READING 1	READING 2
Dry-bulb temperature:	8°C	30°C
Wet-bulb temperature:	6°C	24°C
Difference between dry- and wet-bulb temperatures:	____	____
Dew-point temperature:	____°C	____°C

Table 3 Relative Humidity (percent)*

DRY-BULB TEMPERA-TURE (°C)	Depression of Wet-bulb Temperature (Dry-bulb Temperature − Wet-bulb Temperature = Depression of the Wet Bulb)																					
	1	2	3	4	5	6	7	8	9	10	11	12	13	14	15	16	17	18	19	20	21	22
−20	28																					
−18	40																					
−16	48	0																				
−14	55	11																				
−12	61	23																				
−10	66	33	0																			
−8	71	41	13																			
−6	73	48	20	0																		
−4	77	54	43	11																		
−2	79	58	37	20	1																	
0	81	63	45	28	11																	
2	83	67	51	36	20	6																
4	85	70	56	42	27	14																
6	86	72	59	46	35	22	10	0														
8	87	74	62	51	39	28	17	6														
10	88	76	65	54	43	33	24	13	4													
12	88	78	67	57	48	38	28	19	10	2												
14	89	79	69	60	50	41	33	25	16	8	1											
16	90	80	71	62	54	45	37	29	21	14	7	1										
18	91	81	72	64	56	48	40	33	26	19	12	6	0									
20	91	82	74	66	58	51	44	36	30	23	17	11	5	0								
22	92	83	75	68	60	53	46	40	33	27	21	15	10	4	0							
24	92	84	76	69	62	55	49	42	36	30	25	20	14	9	4	0						
26	92	85	77	70	64	57	51	45	39	34	28	23	18	13	9	5						
28	93	86	78	71	65	59	53	47	42	36	31	26	21	17	12	8	2					
30	93	86	79	72	66	61	55	49	44	39	34	29	25	20	16	12	8	4				
32	93	86	80	73	68	62	56	51	46	41	36	32	27	22	19	14	11	8	4			
34	93	86	81	74	69	63	58	52	48	43	38	34	30	26	22	18	14	11	8	5		
36	94	87	81	75	69	64	59	54	50	44	40	36	32	28	24	21	17	13	10	7	4	
38	94	87	82	76	70	66	60	55	51	46	42	38	34	30	26	23	20	16	13	10	7	
40	94	89	82	76	71	67	61	57	52	48	44	40	36	33	29	25	22	19	16	13	10	7

Relative Humidity Values

Dry-bulb (Air) Temperature

*To determine the relative humidity and dew point, find the air (dry-bulb) temperature on the vertical axis (far left) and the depression of the wet bulb on the horizontal axis (top). Where the two meet, the relative humidity or dew point is found. For example, use a dry-bulb temperature of 20°C and a wet-bulb temperature of 14°C. From Table 3, the relative humidity is 51%, and from Table 4, the dew point is 10°C.

If a psychrometer or hygrometer is available in the laboratory, your instructor will explain the procedure for using the instrument. FOLLOW THE SPECIFIC DIRECTIONS OF YOUR INSTRUCTOR to complete question 27.

27. Use the psychrometer (or hygrometer) to determine the relative humidity and dew-point temperature of the air in the room and outside the building. If you use a psychrometer, record your information in the following spaces.

	ROOM	OUTSIDE
Dry-bulb temperature:	_____	_____
Wet-bulb temperature:	_____	_____
Difference between dry- and wet-bulb temperatures:	_____	_____
Relative humidity:	_____%	_____%
Dew-point temperature:	_____	_____

Table 4 Dew-Point Temperature (°C)*

DRY-BULB TEMPERATURE (°C)	1	2	3	4	5	6	7	8	9	10	11	12	13	14	15	16	17	18	19	20	21	22
−20	−33																					
−18	−28																					
−16	−24																					
−14	−21	−36																				
−12	−18	−28																				
−10	−14	−22																				
−8	−12	−18	−29																			
−6	−10	−14	−22																			
−4	−7	−22	−17	−29																		
−2	−5	−8	−13	−20																		
0	−3	−6	−9	−15	−24																	
2	−1	−3	−6	−11	−17																	
4	1	−1	−4	−7	−11	−19																
6	4	1	−1	−4	−7	−13	−21															
8	6	3	1	−2	−5	−9	−14															
10	8	6	4	1	−2	−5	−9	−14														
12	10	8	6	4	1	−2	−5	−9	−16													
14	12	11	9	6	4	1	−2	−5	−10	−17												
16	14	13	11	9	7	4	1	−1	−6	−10	−17											
18	16	15	13	11	9	7	4	2	−2	−5	−10	−19										
20	19	17	15	14	12	10	7	4	2	−2	−5	−10	−19									
22	21	19	17	16	14	12	10	8	5	3	−1	−5	−10	−19								
24	23	21	20	18	16	14	12	10	8	6	2	−1	−5	−10	−18							
26	25	23	22	20	18	17	15	13	11	9	6	3	0	−4	−9	−18						
28	27	25	24	22	21	19	17	16	14	11	9	7	4	1	−3	−9	−16					
30	29	27	26	24	23	21	19	18	16	14	12	10	8	5	1	−2	−8	−15				
32	31	29	28	27	25	24	22	21	19	17	15	13	11	8	5	2	−2	−7	−14			
34	33	31	30	29	27	26	24	23	21	20	18	16	14	12	9	6	3	−1	−5	−12	−29	
36	35	33	32	31	29	28	27	25	24	22	20	19	17	15	13	10	7	4	0	−4	−10	
38	37	35	34	33	32	30	29	28	26	25	23	21	19	17	15	13	11	8	5	1	−3	−9
40	39	37	36	35	34	32	31	30	28	27	25	24	22	20	18	16	14	12	9	6	2	−2

Header note: *Depression of Wet-bulb Temperature (Dry-bulb Temperature − Wet-bulb Temperature = Depression of the Wet Bulb)*

Dew-Point Temperature Values

*See footnote to Table 3

Condensation

If air is cooled below the dew-point temperature, water will condense (change from vapor to liquid) on available surfaces. In the atmosphere, the particles on which water condenses are called **condensation nuclei**. Condensation may result in the formation of dew or frost on the ground and clouds or fog in the atmosphere.

28. Examine the process of condensation by gradually adding ice to a beaker approximately one-third full of water. As you add the ice, stir the water-ice mixture gently with a thermometer. Note the temperature at the moment water begins to condense on the outside surface of the beaker. After you complete your observations, answer questions 28a and 28b.

a. The temperature at which water began condensing on the outside surface of the beaker was _____.

b. How does the temperature at which water began to condense compare to the dew-point temperature of the air in the room you determined using the psychrometer (or hygrometer)?

_____

29. Refer to Table 2. How many grams of water vapor will condense on a surface if a kilogram of 50°F air with a relative humidity of 100% is cooled to 41°F?

_____ grams of water will condense

30. Assume a kilogram of 25°C air that contains 10 grams of water vapor. Use Table 2. How many grams of water will condense if the air's temperature is lowered to each of the following temperatures?

5°C: _____ grams of condensed water

−10°C: _____ grams of condensed water

31. Considering your answers to the previous questions, what relation exists between the altitude of the base of a cloud, which consists of very small droplets of water, and the dew-point temperature of the air at that altitude?

Daily Temperature and Relative Humidity

Figure 7 shows the typical daily variations in air temperature, relative humidity, and dew-point temperature during two consecutive spring days at a middle latitude city. Use the figure to answer questions 32–36.

32. Relative humidity is at its maximum at (6 A.M., 3 P.M.) on day (1, 2). Circle your answers.

33. The lowest temperature over the two-day period occurs at (6 A.M., noon, 3 P.M.) on day (1, 2).

34. The lowest relative humidity occurs at (6 A.M., noon, 4 P.M.) on day (1, 2).

35. Write a general statement describing the relation between temperature and relative humidity throughout the time period shown in the figure.

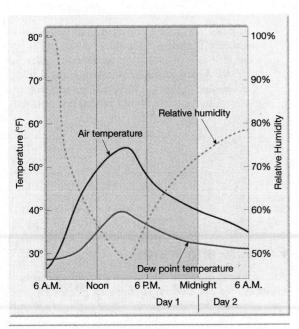

Figure 7 Typical variations in air temperatures, relative humidity, and dew-point temperature during two consecutive spring days at a middle latitude city.

36. Did a dew or frost occur on either of the two days represented in the figure? If so, list when and explain how you arrived at your answer.

Adiabatic Processes

As you have seen, the key to causing water vapor to condense, which is necessary before precipitation can occur, is to reach the dew-point temperature. In nature, when air rises and experiences a decrease in pressure, the air expands and cools. The reverse is also true. Air that is compressed will warm. Temperature changes brought about solely by expansion or compression are called *adiabatic temperature changes*. Air with a temperature above its dew point (unsaturated air) cools by expansion or warms by compression at a rate of 10°C per 1000 meters (1°C per 100 meters) of changing altitude—the **dry adiabatic rate**. After the dew-point temperature is reached, and as condensation occurs, latent heat that has been stored in the water vapor will be liberated. The heat being released by the condensing water slows down the rate of cooling of the air. Rising saturated air will continue to cool by expansion, but at a lesser rate of about 5°C per 1,000 meters (0.5°C per 100 meters) of changing altitude—the **wet adiabatic rate.**

Figure 8 illustrates a kilogram of air at sea level with a temperature of 25°C and a relative humidity of 50%. The air is forced to rise over a 5,000-meter mountain and descend to a plateau 2,000 meters above sea level on the opposite (leeward) side. To help understand the adiabatic process, answer questions 37–49 by referring to Figure 8.

37. What is the saturation mixing ratio, content, and dew-point temperature of the air at sea level?

Saturation mixing ratio: _____g/kg of air

Content: _____g/kg of air

Dew-point temperature: _____°C

38. The air at sea level is (saturated, unsaturated). Circle your answer.

39. The air will initially (warm, cool) as it rises over the windward side of the mountain at the (wet, dry) adiabatic rate, which is (1, 0.5)°C per 100 meters. Circle the correct responses.

40. What will be the air's temperature at 500 meters? _____°C at 500 meters

41. Condensation (will, will not) take place at 500 meters. Circle your answer.

42. The rising air will reach its dew-point temperature at _____ meters and water vapor will begin to (condense, evaporate). Circle your answer.

Figure 8 Adiabatic processes associated with a mountain barrier.

43. From the altitude where condensation begins to occur, to the summit of the mountain, the rising air will continue to expand and will (warm, cool) at the (wet, dry) adiabatic rate of about _____ °C per 100 meters.

44. The temperature of the rising air at the summit of the mountain will be _____ °C.

45. Assuming the air begins to descend on the leeward side of the mountain, it will be compressed and its temperature will (increase, decrease).

46. Assume the relative humidity of the air is below 100% during its entire descent to the plateau. The air will be (saturated, unsaturated) and will warm at the (wet, dry) adiabatic rate of about _____ °C per 100 meters.

47. As the air descends and warms on the leeward side of the mountain, its relative humidity will (increase, decrease).

48. The air's temperature when it reaches the plateau at 2,000 meters will be _____ °C.

49. Explain why mountains might cause dry conditions on their leeward sides.

_____

_____

Global Patterns of Precipitation

Use Figure 9 to answer questions 50–54.

50. List at least four areas of the world that receive the greatest average annual (over 160 cm) precipitation.

_____

_____

51. The polar regions of Earth have (high, low) average annual precipitation. Circle your answer.

52. What is the average annual precipitation at your location?

_____ centimeters per year, which is equivalent to _____ inches per year.

53. Describe the pattern of average annual precipitation in North America.

_____

_____

_____

54. The inset in Figure 9 illustrates the variability, or reliability, of the precipitation in Africa. After you compare the inset to the annual precipitation map for Africa, summarize the relation between the amount of precipitation an area receives and the variability, or reliability, of that precipitation.

_____

_____

_____

Pressure and Wind

Atmospheric pressure and wind are two elements of weather that are closely interrelated. Although pressure is the element least noticed by people in a weather report, it is pressure differences in the atmosphere that drive the winds that often bring changes in temperature and moisture.

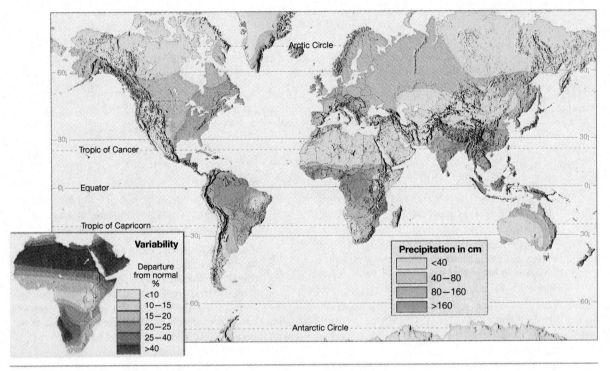

Figure 9   Average annual precipitation in centimeters.

Atmospheric Pressure

Atmospheric pressure is the force exerted by the weight of the atmosphere. It varies over the face of Earth, primarily because of temperature differences. Typically, warm air is less dense than cool air and, therefore, exerts less pressure. Cold, dense air is often associated with higher pressures. Pressure also changes with altitude.

The instrument used to determine atmospheric pressure is the **barometer** (Figure 10). Two units that can be used to measure air pressure are *inches of mercury* and *millibars*. Inches of mercury refers to the height to which a column of mercury will rise in a glass tube that has been inverted into a reservoir of mercury. The millibar is a unit that measures the actual force of the atmosphere pushing down on a surface. Standard pressure at sea level is 29.92 inches of mercury or 1,013.2 millibars (Figure 11). A pressure greater than 29.92 inches or 1,013.2 millibars is called *high pressure*. A pressure less than the standards is called *low pressure*.

55. If a barometer is located in the laboratory, record the current atmospheric pressure in both inches of mercury and millibars. If necessary, use Figure 11 to convert the units.

Inches of mercury: _____ inches of mercury

Millibars: _____ millibars (mb)

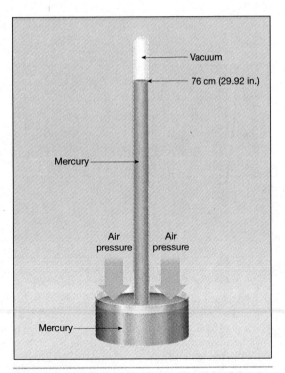

Figure 10   Simple mercury barometer. The weight of the column of mercury is balanced by the pressure exerted on the dish of mercury by the air above. If the pressure decreases, the column of mercury falls; if the pressure increases, the column rises.

PRESSURE

| | Strong low pressure system (cyclone) | Standard sea level pressure | Strong high pressure system (anticyclone) |

millibars 956 960 964 968 972 976 980 984 988 992 996 1000 1004 1008 1012 1016 1020 1024 1028 1032 1036 1040 1044 1048 1052 1056

inches 28.2   28.4   28.6   28.8   29.0   29.2   29.4   29.6   29.8   30.0   30.2   30.4   30.6   30.8   31.0   31.2

Figure 11   Scale for comparing pressure readings in millibars and inches of mercury. (After NOAA)

Use Figure 12, showing generalized pressure variations with altitude, to answer questions 56 and 57.

56. Atmospheric pressure (increases, decreases) with an increase in altitude because there is (more, less) atmosphere above to exert a force. Circle your answers.

57. Pressure changes with altitude (most, least) rapidly near Earth's surface.

Since surface elevations vary, barometric readings are adjusted to indicate what the pressure would be if the barometer was located at sea level. This provides a common standard for mapping pressure, regardless of elevation.

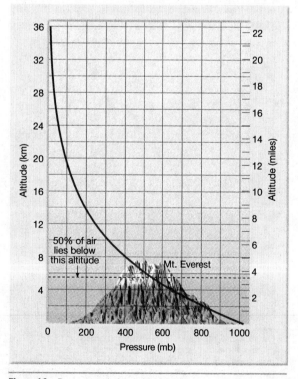

Figure 12   Pressure variations with altitude.

58. A city that is 200 meters above sea level would (add, subtract) units to its barometric reading in order to correct its pressure to sea level.

Observe the average global surface pressure maps with associated winds for January and July in Figure 13. The lines shown are **isobars**, which connect points of equal barometric pressure, adjusted to sea level. Isobars can be used to identify the principal pressure zones on Earth, which include the **equatorial lows**, **subtropical highs**, and **subpolar lows**. Answer questions 59–65 using Figure 13.

59. The units used on the maps to indicate pressure are (inches of mercury, millibars). Circle your answer.

60. By writing the word "HIGH" or "LOW," indicate on the maps the general pressure at each of the following latitudes: 60°N, 30°N, 0°, 30°S, 60°S.

61. Write on the maps the names (equatorial low, subtropical high, or subpolar low) of each of the pressure zones you identified in question 60.

62. During the summer months, January in the Southern Hemisphere and July in the Northern Hemisphere, (high, low) pressure is more common over land. Circle your answer.

63. (High, Low) pressure is most associated with the land in the winter months.

64. Considering what you know about the unequal heating of land and water and the influence of air temperature on pressure, why does the pressure over continents change with the seasons?

_____

_____

65. Why does the air over the oceans maintain a more uniform pressure throughout the year?

_____

_____

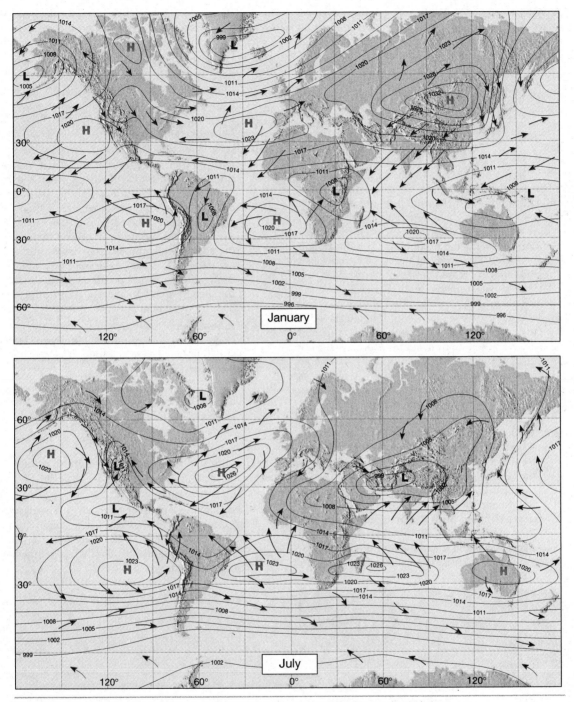

Figure 13   Average surface barometric pressure in millibars for January and July with associated winds.

The differential heating and cooling of land and water over most of Earth causes the zones of pressure to be broken into cells of pressure. Pressure cells are shown on a map as a system of closed, concentric isobars. **High pressure cells**, called **anticyclones**, are typically associated with descending (subsiding) air. **Low pressure cells**, called **cyclones**, have rising air in their centers. Lo-

cate and examine some of the pressure cells on the maps in Figure 13. Then answer questions 66 and 67.

66. In an anticyclone, the (highest, lowest) pressure occurs at the center of the cell. In a cyclone, the (highest, lowest) pressure occurs at the center. Circle your answers.

67. With which pressure cell, anticyclone or cyclone, would the vertical movement of air be most favorable for cloud formation and precipitation? Explain your answer with reference to the adiabatic process.

_____

_____

Wind

The horizontal movement of air is called **wind**. Wind is initiated because of horizontal pressure differences. Air flows from areas of higher pressure to areas of lower pressure. The direction of the wind is influenced by the **Coriolis effect** and friction between the air and Earth's surface. The velocity of the wind is controlled by the difference in pressure between two areas.

All free-moving objects or fluids, including the wind, experience the Coriolis effect and have their paths deflected. However, the deflection, which is due to the Earth's rotation about an axis, is only apparent as an observer watching from space would see the object's path as a straight line. To better understand how the Coriolis effect influences the motion of objects as they move across Earth's surface, conduct the following experiment by completing the indicated steps.

Step 1: Working in groups of two or more, construct a rotating "table" that represents Earth's surface by first taping a thumbtack upside down on the table top (or inserting it through a piece of cardboard). Next, center a sheet of heavyweight paper or thin cardboard over the point of the tack and push the sharp end of the tack through the paper (Figure 14). Turning the paper about the thumbtack represents the rotating Earth viewed from above the pole.

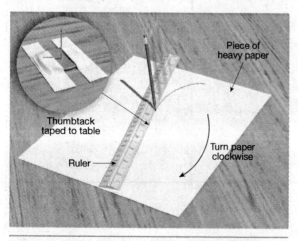

Figure 14 Coriolis experiment setup—Southern Hemisphere.

Step 2: Place a straight edge (a 12-inch ruler will do) across the paper, resting it on the sharp point of the thumbtack.

Step 3: Using the straight edge as a guide and beginning at the edge nearest you, draw a straight line across the entire piece of paper. Mark the beginning of the line you drew with an arrow pointing in the direction the pencil moved. Label the line "no rotation."

Step 4: Now have one person hold the straight edge and another turn the paper *counterclockwise* (the direction the Earth rotates when viewed from above the North Pole) about the thumbtack. Using a different color pencil than you used in Step 3, while spinning the paper at a slow constant speed, draw a second line along the edge of the straight edge across the rotating paper. Mark the beginning of the line you drew with an arrow pointing in the direction the pencil moved. Label the resulting line "Northern Hemisphere."

Step 5: Repeat Step 4, only this time rotate the paper *clockwise* (representing the Southern Hemisphere). Label the resulting line "Southern Hemisphere."

Step 6: Repeat Step 4 several times, varying the speed of rotation of the paper with each trial. Identify each new line by labeling it either "slow," "fast," or "very fast."

Questions 68 through 70 refer to the Coriolis experiment.

68. Describe the apparent path of a free-moving object over Earth's surface on a "nonrotating" Earth, the Northern Hemisphere (counterclockwise rotation), and the Southern Hemisphere (clockwise rotation).

_____

_____

_____

_____

_____

69. In the Northern Hemisphere, the deflection of objects is to the (right, left), while in the Southern Hemisphere it is to the (right, left). Circle your answers.

70. Summarize your observations of the relation between speed of rotation and magnitude of the Coriolis effect you observed in **Step 6.**

_____

_____

_____

From your observations in **Step 6,** you would suspect that the deflection in the path of a free-moving object would be maximized near the equator where Earth's rotational velocity is greatest. However, it is NOT. Vector motion on the surface of a sphere is complex; however, the Coriolis effect is controlled primarily by rotation about a VERTICAL axis. In your experiment, all points on the paper were rotating about a vertical axis, the thumbtack. However, the flat paper does not represent the "real" spherical Earth. On Earth, the vertical axis of rotation is a line connecting the geographic poles that is only vertical to Earth's surface at each pole. On the Equator, the axis is _parallel_ to the surface; therefore, there is no rotation about a vertical axis. As a consequence, the Coriolis effect is strongest at the poles and weakens equatorward, becoming nonexistent at the equator. (To help visualize this changing orientation, obtain a globe and hold a pencil parallel to Earth's axis at the North Pole. Notice the axis is vertical to the surface, just as in the experiment. Now, _while keeping the pencil parallel to Earth's axis of rotation,_ slowly move it over the surface to the equator. Notice how the orientation of the pencil changes relative to the surface as it is moved. At the equator, the pencil is now parallel to the surface and rotation about the pencil is directed toward and away from Earth's center, not over the surface.)

71. Considering what you have learned about the Coriolis effect, write a brief statement describing the Coriolis effect on the atmosphere of the planet Venus, about the same size as Earth, but with a period of rotation of 244 Earth days. What about on Jupiter, a planet much larger than Earth, with a 10-hour day?

_____

_____

_____

_____

Examine the global wind pattern (shown with arrows) that is associated with the global pattern of pressure in Figure 13. The wind arrows can be used to identify the global wind belts, which include the **trade winds, westerlies,** and **polar easterlies.** Then answer questions 72–75.

72. Examine the pressure cells in Figure 13. Then, on Figure 15, complete the diagrams of the indicated pressure cells for each hemisphere. Label the isobars with appropriate pressures _and_ use arrows to indicate the surface air movement in each pressure cell.

73. In the following spaces, indicate the movements of air in high and low pressure cells for each hemisphere. Write one of the two choices given in italics for each blank.

	NORTHERN HEMISPHERE		SOUTHERN HEMISPHERE	
	HIGH	LOW	HIGH	LOW
Surface air moves _into_ or _out of:_	___	___	___	___
Surface air will _rise_ or _subside_ in the center:	___	___	___	___
Surface air motion is _clockwise_ or _counterclockwise:_	___	___	___	___

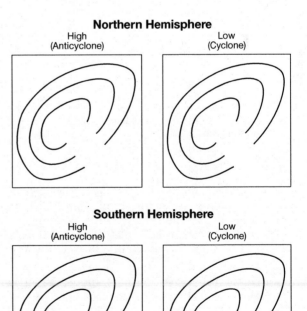

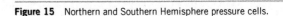

Figure 15 Northern and Southern Hemisphere pressure cells.

Figure 16 Global winds (generalized).

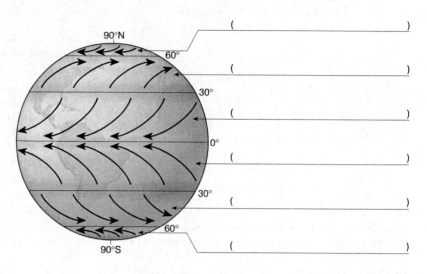

WIND BELT

90°N
60°
30°
0°
30°
60°
90°S

( )
( )
( )
( )
( )
( )

74. Write a brief statement that describes the difference in surface air movement between a Northern Hemisphere and Southern Hemisphere anticyclone.

_____
_____
_____

75. Write the name of each global wind belt (trade winds, westerlies, or polar easterlies) at the appropriate location on Figure 16. Also indicate by name each global wind belt on the world maps in Figure 13.

In Figure 13, notice the seasonal changes in wind direction, called **monsoons**, over continents.

76. During the (summer, winter) season, the air is moving from the continent to the ocean. Circle your answer.

77. During the (summer, winter) season, the air is moving from the ocean to the continent.

78. In what way is the seasonal change in wind direction over continents related to pressure?

_____
_____

79. What effect will the seasonal reversal of wind have on moisture in the air and the potential for precipitation over the continents during the following seasons?

Summer season: _____
_____

Winter season: _____
_____

By examining Figure 13, you should notice that the systems of pressure belts and global winds change latitude with the seasons.

80. In what manner is the seasonal shift in pressure belts and global winds related to the movement of the overhead noon Sun throughout the year?

_____

Atmospheric Moisture, Pressure, and Wind on the Internet

Using what you have learned in this exercise, investigate the current weather conditions at your location and in North America by completing the corresponding online activity on the *Applications & Investigations in Earth Science* website at http://prenhall.com/earthsciencelab

Atmospheric Moisture, Pressure, and Wind

Date Due: _____

Name: _____

Date: _____

Class: _____

After you have finished this exercise, complete the following questions. You may have to refer to the exercise for assistance or to locate specific answers. Be prepared to submit this summary/report to your instructor at the designated time.

1. Answer the following by circling the correct response.

   a. Liquid water changes to water vapor by the process called (condensation, evaporation, deposition).

   b. (Warm, Cold) air has the greatest saturation mixing ratio.

   c. Lowering the air temperature will (increase, decrease) the relative humidity.

   d. At the dew-point temperature, the relative humidity is (25%, 50%, 75%, 100%).

   e. When condensation occurs, heat is (absorbed, released) by water vapor.

   f. Rising air (warms, cools) by (expansion, compression).

   g. In the early morning hours when the daily air temperature is often coolest, relative humidity is generally at its (lowest, highest).

2. What is the dew-point temperature of a kilogram of air when a psychrometer measures an 8°C dry-bulb temperature and a 6°C wet-bulb reading?

   Dew-point temperature = _____ °C

3. Explain the principle that governs the operation of a psychrometer for determining relative humidity.

   _____

   _____

   _____

4. Describe the adiabatic process and how it is responsible for causing condensation in the atmosphere.

   _____

   _____

   _____

5. In the section of the exercise "Adiabatic Processes," question 42, what was the altitude where condensation occurred as the air was rising over the mountain?

   _____ meters

6. Place each of the following statements in proper sequence (1 for the first) leading to the development of clouds.

   _____: dew-point temperature reached

   _____: air begins to rise

   _____: condensation occurs

   _____: adiabatic cooling

7. Assume a parcel of air on the surface with a temperature of 29°C and a relative humidity of 50%. If the parcel rises, at what altitude should clouds form?

   _____

8. Describe the Coriolis effect and its influence in both the Northern and Southern Hemispheres.

   _____

   _____

85

PRESSURE ZONE   WIND BELT

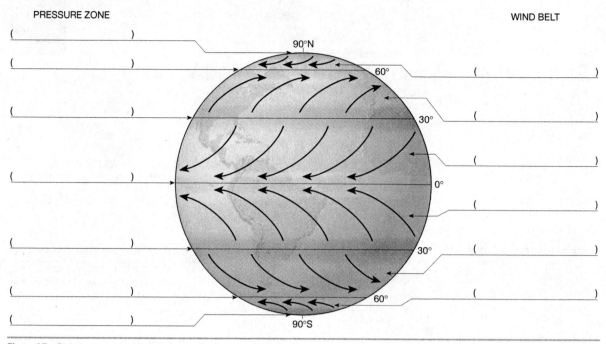

Figure 17 Global pressures and winds (generalized).

9. Refer to Figure 17. Use the indicated parallels of latitude as a guide to write the names of the global pressure zones and wind belts at their proper locations.

10. On Figure 18, illustrate, by labeling the isobars, a typical Northern Hemisphere cyclone and anticyclone. Use arrows to indicate the movement of surface air associated with each pressure cell.

11. Complete Figure 19 by using the indicated surface barometric pressures to assist in drawing appropriate isobars. Begin with the 988 mb isobar and use a 4 mb interval between successive isobars.

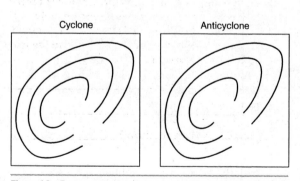

Figure 18 Pressures and winds in a typical Northern Hemisphere cyclone and anticyclone.

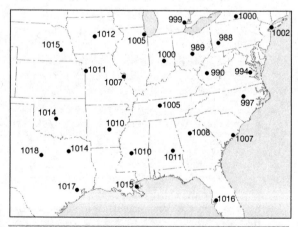

Figure 19 Atmospheric pressures for select cities.

7

Global Climates

No investigation of the atmosphere is complete without examining the global distribution of the major atmospheric elements. To help understand this worldwide diversity, scientists have devised a variety of classification systems that simplify and describe the general weather conditions that occur at various places on Earth.

This exercise investigates world climates using the system of climate classification devised by Wladimir Köppen (1846–1940). Climographs for several climatic types will be prepared and the global distribution of climates will be examined (Figure 1).

Objectives

After you have completed this exercise, you should be able to:

1. Understand the nature of classification systems.
2. Read and prepare a climograph.
3. List the criteria used to define each principal climatic type.
4. Describe the general location of each principal climate group.

Materials

ruler
calculator

Materials Supplied by Your Instructor

world map or atlas

Terms

climate   Köppen system
climatology   climograph

Climate

Climate may be defined as the synthesis, or summary, of weather conditions at a particular place over a long period of time. Climatic classification simplifies the complex distribution of the weather elements for analysis and explanation.

Climatology involves grouping those areas that have similar weather characteristics. Temperature and precipitation are the two elements most commonly used in climate classifications. However, other methods, using different criteria, have also been developed. It should be remembered that any classification is artificial, and its value depends on the intended use.

Examining Global Temperatures

Temperature is one of the most essential elements in any climate classification. Completing questions 1–3 using the temperature data in Table 1 will help you gain a better understanding of the relationship between location and temperature.

1. Stations 1–3 in Table 1 are representative of three North American cities at approximately 40° North latitude. Choose which station represents each of the following locations, and give the reason for your selection.

   Interior of the continent? _____

   _____

   West coast of the continent? _____

   _____

   East coast of the continent? _____

   _____

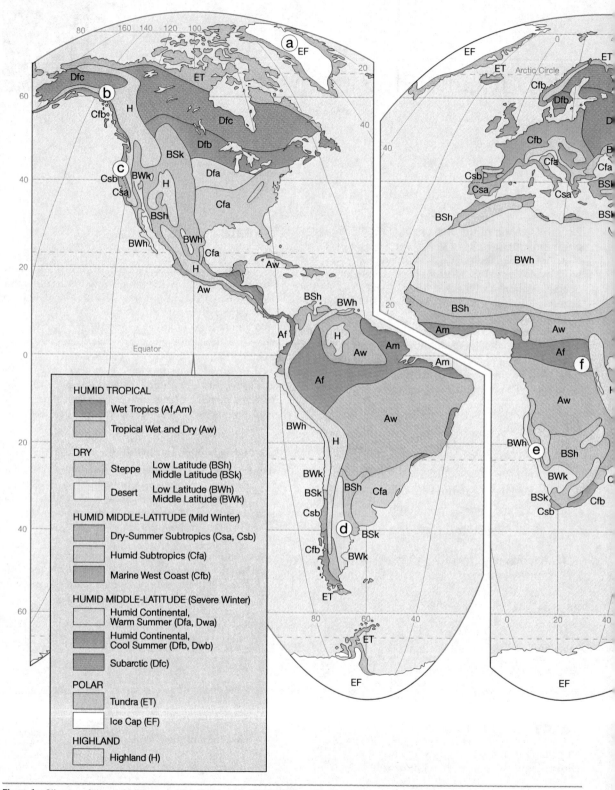

Figure 1   Climates of the world (Köppen). (Adapted from E. Willard Miller, *Physical Geography,* Columbus, Ohio, Macmillan/Merrill, 1985. Plate 2)

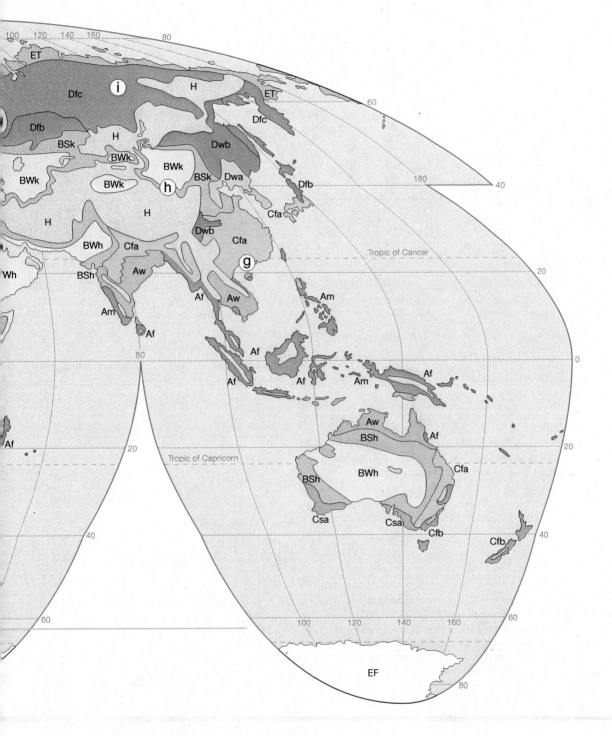

Table 1   **Annual Temperature Data (°F)**

STATION	J	F	M	A	M	J	J	A	S	O	N	D	ANNUAL MEAN
1	25	28	36	48	61	72	75	74	66	55	39	28	50
2	48	48	49	50	54	55	57	57	57	54	52	49	52
3	31	31	38	49	60	69	74	73	69	59	44	35	52
4	25	26	35	45	58	70	75	72	65	55	45	35	50
5	20	34	38	46	51	54	60	53	49	40	32	25	40
6	42	48	50	55	56	58	59	60	59	56	48	46	51
7	76	76	76	76	78	78	77	77	76	75	74	74	76
8	90	88	84	79	77	73	70	71	76	79	82	87	80
9	−2	11	25	36	48	54	70	60	50	36	18	10	34
10	59	58	59	59	60	58	60	59	60	58	59	60	59
11	70	69	69	66	61	57	56	60	66	70	71	70	66
12	−46	−35	−10	16	41	59	66	60	42	16	−21	−41	12
13	22	25	37	51	62	72	77	75	66	54	39	27	50
14	82	82	82	83	83	82	82	83	83	83	82	83	83
15	27	30	34	41	48	54	57	55	50	43	36	31	42
16	40	44	48	54	61	69	77	76	67	57	47	41	57

2. Selecting from Stations 4–10, answer questions 2a–c.

   a. Station _____ is in the Southern Hemisphere.

   b. Station _____ must be a high-altitude location.

   c. Which station(s) must be quite close to the equator? Why?

   _____

3. Match each of Stations 11–16 with its most likely location by selecting the corresponding lower-case letter (a–i) on the world map, Figure 1.

   Station 11: letter _____   Station 14: letter _____

   Station 12: letter _____   Station 15: letter _____

   Station 13: letter _____   Station 16: letter _____

Using a Climograph

Temperature and precipitation are presented on a **climograph** such as the one shown in Figure 2. Average monthly temperatures are connected with a single line and read from the temperature scale on the left axis. Average precipitation for each month is represented with a bar or line and read from the precipitation scale on the right axis.

Refer to the climograph, Figure 2, to answer questions 4–9. Circle the correct response.

4. At the place represented by the climograph, the month of (May, June, January) receives the greatest amount of precipitation.

5. The lowest temperature occurs during the month of (July, December, January).

6. The approximate average annual temperature is (0, 10, 20)°C.

7. The total annual precipitation is approximately (240, 480, 720) millimeters.

8. The place represented by the climograph is in the (Northern, Southern) Hemisphere.

9. The (summer, winter) months receive the greatest amount of precipitation.

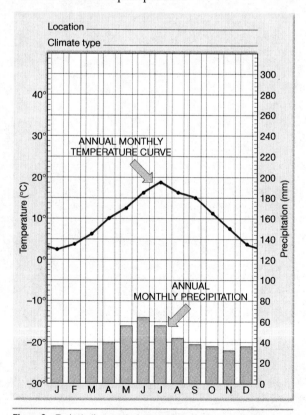

Location _____

Climate type _____

Figure 2   Typical climograph. Letters along the bottom margin represent the months. Average monthly temperatures (°C) are plotted with a single line using the scale on the left axis. Precipitation for each month (in mm) is plotted with a bar using the right axis.

The Nature of Classification

Classification by its nature is an artificial endeavor designed to simplify a large amount of data into manageable units. To accomplish this, decisions must be made as to which criteria and limits best serve the purpose of the classification. Completing questions 10–12 using the climographs in Figure 3 will give you some insight into the nature of conceiving a classification scheme.

10. Working in groups of 4 or 5, develop the best possible classification scheme for the stations represented by the climographs in Figure 3 by arranging them into groups with similar characteristics. When you have finished, describe your classification system, listing the criteria you established. (*Note:* Making a copy of Figure 3 and cutting out individual stations may make it easier to visualize different classification arrangements.)

_____

_____

_____

_____

_____

_____

11. Why is the classification scheme you presented in question 10 better than other possible systems you considered?

_____

_____

_____

_____

_____

12. Compare the classification system your group devised with the systems developed by two other groups. Which is the best classification scheme? Why?

_____

_____

_____

_____

_____

_____

_____

_____

_____

_____

Köppen System of Climatic Classification

Table 2 presents the climatic classification system devised by Wladimir Köppen. Since its introduction, the **Köppen system**, with some modification, has become the best-known and most-used classification for presenting the general world pattern of climates.

The Köppen system of climatic classification employs five principal climate groups. Four of the groups are defined on the basis of temperature characteristics and the fifth has precipitation as its primary criterion. Further division of the groups into climatic types allows for a more detailed climatic description. Köppen believed that the distribution of natural vegetation was the best expression of the totality of climate. Therefore, the boundaries he chose were based largely on the limits of certain plant associations. Before you proceed, examine Table 2 closely.

13. On Table 3, list the names and general characteristics of each principal climate group next to its designated classification letter. Use Table 2 as a reference.

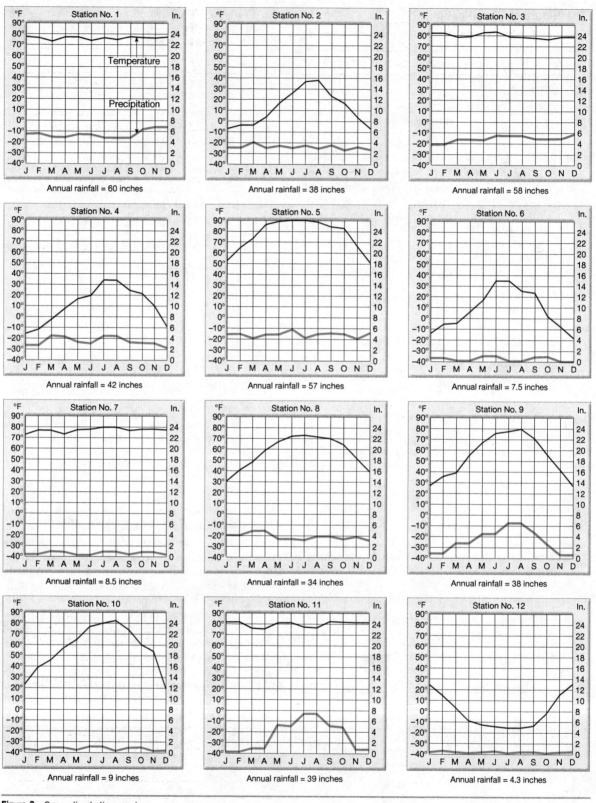

Figure 3 Generalized climographs.

Table 2 Köppen System of Climatic Classification

NAME	LETTER SYMBOL			CHARACTERISTICS
	1ST	2ND	3RD	
Humid Tropical (type A) Climates	A			Average temperature of the coldest month is 18°C or higher
		f		Every month has 6 cm of precipitation or more
		m		Short dry season; precipitation in driest month less than 6 cm but equal to or greater than $10 - R/25$ (R is the annual rainfall in cm)
		w		Well-defined winter dry season; precipitation in driest month less than $10 - R/25$
		s		Well-defined summer dry season (rare)
Dry (type B) Climates	B			Potential evaporation exceeds precipitation. The dry–humid boundary is defined by the following formulas: (Note: R is average annual precipitation in cm and T is average annual temperature in °C) $R < 2T + 28$ when 70% or more of rain falls in warmer 6 months $R < 2T$ when 70% or more of rain falls in cooler 6 months $R < 2T + 14$ when neither half year has 70% or more of rain
		S		Steppe ⎤
				The BS–BW boundary is 1/2 the dry–humid boundary
		W		Desert ⎦
			h	Average annual temperature is 18°C or greater
			k	Average annual temperature is less than 18°C
Humid Middle-Latitude with Mild Winters (type C) Climates	C			Average temperature of the coldest month is under 18°C and above −3°C
		w		At least ten times as much precipitation in a summer month as in the driest winter month
		s		At least three times as much precipitation in a winter month as in the driest summer month; precipitation in driest summer month less than 4 cm
		f		Criteria for w and s cannot be met
			a	Warmest month is over 22°C; at least 4 months over 10°C
			b	No month above 22°C; at least 4 months over 10°C
			c	One to 3 months above 10°C
Humid Middle-Latitude with Severe Winters (type D) Climates	D			Average temperature of coldest month is −3°C or below; average temperature of warmest month is greater than 10°C
		s		Same as under C climates
		w		Same as under C climates
		f		Same as under C climates
			a	Same as under C climates
			b	Same as under C climates
			c	Same as under C climates
			d	Average temperature of the coldest month is −38°C or below
Polar (type E) Climates	E			Average temperature of the warmest month is below 10°C
		T		Average temperature of the warmest month is greater than 0°C and less than 10°C
		F		Average temperature of the warmest month is 0°C or below

Table 3 Characteristics of the Principal Climate Groups

CLIMATE GROUP	NAME	TEMPERATURE AND/OR PRECIPITATION CHARACTERISTICS
A:	_____	_____
B:	_____	_____
C:	_____	_____
D:	_____	_____
E:	_____	_____

Table 4 **Climatic Data for Representative Stations**

	J	F	M	A	M	J	J	A	S	O	N	D	YEAR
					IQUITOS, PERU (AF); LAT. 3°39'S; 115 M								
Temp. (°C)	25.6	25.6	24.4	25.0	24.4	23.3	23.3	24.4	24.4	25.0	25.6	25.6	24.7
Precip. (mm)	259	249	310	165	254	188	168	117	221	183	213	292	2619
					RIO DE JANEIRO, BRAZIL (AW); LAT. 22°50'S; 26 M								
Temp. (°C)	25.9	26.1	25.2	23.9	22.3	21.3	20.8	21.1	21.5	22.3	23.1	24.4	23.2
Precip. (mm)	137	137	143	116	73	43	43	43	53	74	97	127	1086
					FAYA, CHAD (BWH); LAT. 18°00'N; 251 M								
Temp. (°C)	20.4	22.7	27.0	30.6	33.8	34.2	33.6	32.7	32.6	30.5	25.5	21.3	28.7
Precip. (mm)	0	0	0	0	0	2	1	11	2	0	0	0	16
					SALT LAKE CITY, UTAH (BSK); LAT. 40°46'N; 1288 M								
Temp. (°C)	−2.1	0.9	4.7	9.9	14.7	19.4	24.7	23.6	18.3	11.5	3.4	−0.2	10.7
Precip. (mm)	34	30	40	45	36	25	15	22	13	29	33	31	353
					WASHINGTON, D.C. (CFA); LAT. 38°50'N; 20 M								
Temp. (°C)	2.7	3.2	7.1	13.2	18.8	23.4	25.7	24.7	20.9	15.0	8.7	3.4	13.9
Precip. (mm)	77	63	82	80	105	82	105	124	97	78	72	71	1036
					BREST, FRANCE (CFB); LAT. 48°24'N; 103 M								
Temp. (°C)	6.1	5.8	7.8	9.2	11.6	14.4	15.6	16.0	14.7	12.0	9.0	7.0	10.8
Precip. (mm)	133	96	83	69	68	56	62	80	87	104	138	150	1126
					ROME, ITALY (CSA); LAT. 41°52'N; 3 M								
Temp. (°C)	8.0	9.0	10.9	13.7	17.5	21.6	24.4	24.2	21.5	17.2	12.7	9.5	15.9
Precip. (mm)	83	73	52	50	48	18	9	18	70	110	113	105	749
					PEORIA, ILLINOIS (DFA); LAT. 40°45'N; 180 M								
Temp. (°C)	−4.4	−2.2	4.4	10.6	16.7	21.7	23.9	22.7	18.3	11.7	3.8	−2.2	10.4
Precip. (mm)	46	51	69	84	99	97	97	81	97	61	61	51	894
					VERKHOYANSK, RUSSIA (DFD); LAT. 67°33'N; 137 M								
Temp. (°C)	−46.8	−43.1	−30.2	−13.5	2.7	12.9	15.7	11.4	2.7	−14.3	−35.7	−44.5	−15.2
Precip. (mm)	7	5	5	4	5	25	33	30	13	11	10	7	155
					IVIGTUT, GREENLAND (ET); LAT. 61°12'N; 129 M								
Temp. (°C)	−7.2	−7.2	−4.4	−0.6	4.4	8.3	10.0	8.3	5.0	1.1	−3.3	−6.1	0.7
Precip. (mm)	84	66	86	62	89	81	79	94	150	145	117	79	1132
					MCMURDO STATION, ANTARCTICA (EF); LAT. 77°53'S; 2 M								
Temp. (°C)	−4.4	−8.9	−15.5	−22.8	−23.9	−24.4	−26.1	−26.1	−24.4	−18.8	−10.0	−3.9	−17.4
Precip. (mm)	13	18	10	10	10	8	5	8	10	5	5	8	110

Table 4 contains climatic data for several stations that are representative of Köppen climatic types. Use the data in Tables 2 and 4 to answer the following questions.

Humid Tropical (type A) Climates

With the exception of the dry climates, no other climate covers as large an area on Earth as the humid tropical climates.

14. What temperature criterion is used for defining an A climate?

_____

15. Plot the monthly temperature and precipitation data for Iquitos, Peru, an A climate, given in Table 4 on the climate chart, Figure 4.

Use the Iquitos, Peru, climograph you prepared in question 15 to answer questions 16–19.

16. What is the *annual temperature range* (difference between highest and lowest monthly temperatures) for Iquitos?

_____ °C

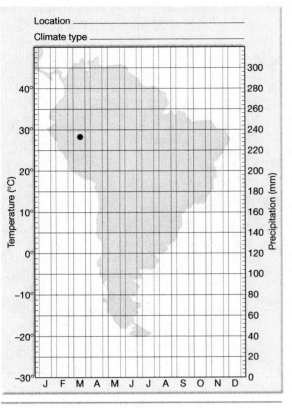

Location _____

Climate type _____

Figure 4 Climograph for Iquitos, Peru.

17. Describe the yearly variability of temperature for A climates.

_____

18. Notice that Iquitos receives an average of 2,619 mm of precipitation per year. How many inches of precipitation per year would this equal? (*Hint:* You may have to refer to the conversion tables located on the inside back cover of this manual.)

    2,619 mm equals _____ inches

19. The precipitation at Iquitos is (concentrated in one season, distributed throughout the year). Circle your answer.

    Use the world climate map, Figure 1, to answer questions 20–22.

20. In what latitude belt are A climates located?

_____

21. The most extensive areas of tropical rain forest (Af) climates are located (along coasts, in the interiors) of continents. Circle your answer.

22. Considering the locations of A climates, would weather fronts or columns of rapidly rising, hot surface air be most likely responsible for the precipitation? Explain your answer.

_____

_____

Dry (type B) Climates

Of all the climate groups, the dry climates cover the greatest portion of Earth's surface. To be classified as a dry climate does not necessarily imply little or no precipitation, but rather indicates that the yearly precipitation is not as great as the potential loss of moisture by evaporation.

23. What are three variables that the Köppen classification uses to establish the boundary between dry and humid climates?

    1) _____

    2) _____

    3) _____

24. What name is applied to the following climatic types?

    BW: _____

    BS: _____

25. What is the primary cause of arid climates in the tropics?

_____

26. What factors contribute to the formation of arid climates in the middle latitudes?

_____

_____

    To answer questions 27 and 28, refer to the world climate map, Figure 1.

27. At what latitudes, North and South, are the most extensive arid areas located?

_____

28. The Sahara desert in northern Africa is the largest area in the world with a BWh climate. What are some other regions that have the same climate?

_____

Humid Middle-Latitude Climates with Mild Winters (type C)

A large percentage of the world's population is located in areas with C climates. It is a climate characterized by weather contrasts brought about by changing seasons. On the average, the regions of C climates are dominated by contrasting air masses and associated middle-latitude cyclones.

29. What temperature criterion is used to define the boundary of C climates?

_____

30. Using the data in Table 4, on Figure 5, prepare climographs for Washington, D.C., and Rome, Italy.

    Answer questions 31–34 using the climographs you have constructed for Washington, D.C., and Rome, Italy, Figure 5.

31. In what manner are the temperature curves for each of the two cities similar?

_____

32. How does the annual distribution of precipitation vary between the two cities?

_____

33. What is the difference between a Cf (Washington, D.C.) climate and a Cs (Rome, Italy) climate?

_____

_____

34. (Weather fronts, Columns of rapidly rising, hot surface air) are most likely responsible for the winter precipitation in Cf climates. Circle your answer.

    Use the world climate map, Figure 1, to answer questions 35–37.

35. What countries in Asia have areas of climate similar to that of Washington, D.C.?

_____

36. What Southern Hemisphere countries have climates similar to that of Washington, D.C.?

_____

37. Which U.S. state has a climate similar to that of Rome, Italy?

_____

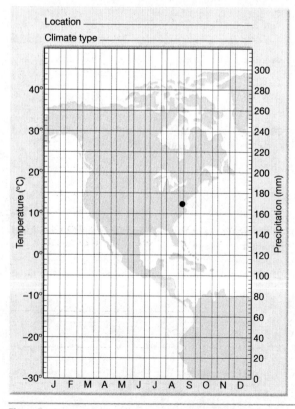
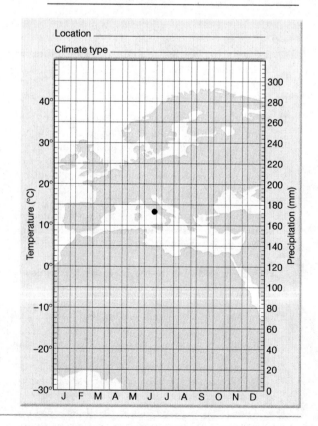

Figure 5 Climographs for Washington, D.C., and Rome, Italy.

Humid Middle-Latitude Climates with Severe Winters (type D)

The harsh winters and relatively short growing season restrict agricultural activity in much of the area of D climates. The northern portions of D climate regions are covered by coniferous forests, with lumbering being a significant economic activity.

38. What criteria are used for defining a D climate?

_____

_____

39. Use the data from Table 4 to plot a climograph for Peoria, Illinois, on Figure 6.

Use the climograph you have constructed for Peoria, Illinois, Figure 6, to answer questions 40–42.

40. What is the annual range of temperature in Peoria, Illinois?

_____°C

41. How does the annual range of temperature in Peoria, Illinois, compare to the temperature ranges in Iquitos, Peru, and Rome, Italy?

_____

_____

_____

_____

_____

42. During what season does Peoria receive its greatest precipitation and how does this compare with the seasonal distribution of precipitation for Rome, Italy?

_____

_____

_____

_____

_____

Use the world climate map, Figure 1, to answer questions 43–45.

43. Which continent has the greatest continuous expanse of D climates?

_____

44. D climates are located only in the (Northern, Southern) Hemisphere. Circle your answer.

45. Suggest a reason why D climates are located in only the hemisphere you selected in question 44.

_____

_____

_____

_____

_____

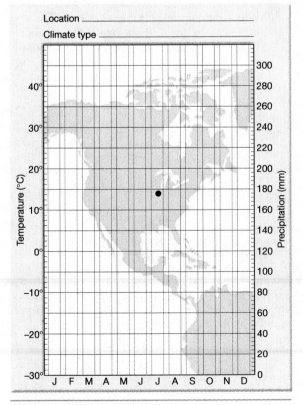

Figure 6 Climograph for Peoria, Illinois.

Table 5   Climatic Data for Quito, Ecuador

	J	F	M	A	M	J	J	A	S	O	N	D	YEAR
	QUITO, ECUADOR LAT. 0°, LONG. 79°W; 2770 M												
Temp. (°C)	13	13	13	13	13	13	13	14	14	13	13	13	13
Precip. (mm)	99	110	142	175	137	43	20	30	69	113	95	93	1126

Polar (type E) Climates

The polar climates, found at high latitudes and scattered high altitudes in mountains, are regions of cold temperatures and sparse population. Low evaporation rates allow these areas to be classified as humid, even though the annual precipitation is modest.

46. What criterion is used for defining E climates?

47. Contrast the characteristics and locations of the two basic polar climates.

    ET climates: _____

    _____

    _____

    EF climates: _____

    _____

    _____

Climate and Altitude

Although often not included with the principal climate groups, *high-altitude*, or *highland* (type H) climates exist in all climatic regions. They are the result of the changes in radiation, temperature, humidity, precipitation, and atmospheric pressure that take place with elevation and orientation of mountain slopes.

    Examine the climatic data for Quito, Ecuador, in Table 5. Quito is located in a region where A climates are expected. However, its altitude of 2,770 meters (9,086 feet) changes its Köppen classification.

48. Use Table 5 and Table 2 to determine the climatic classification of Quito, Ecuador.

    Climate of Quito, Ecuador: _____

    Criteria used for the selection of the climate type of Quito, Ecuador: _____

    _____

    _____

49. Locate Quito, Ecuador, on a map or globe. Considering its location, what effect has altitude had on the climatic classification?

    _____

    _____

50. Why would you expect the vegetation in the area of Quito to be different from that found at Guayaquil, Ecuador, a city located on the coast?

    _____

    _____

51. From Figure 1, where is the greatest continuous expanse of high-altitude (highland) climate located?

    _____

    _____

Climate on the Internet

Continue your analysis of the topics presented in this exercise by completing the corresponding online activity on the *Applications & Investigations in Earth Science* website at http://prenhall.com/earthsciencelab

Global Climates

Date Due: _____

Name: _____
Date: _____
Class: _____

After you have finished this exercise, complete the following questions. You may have to refer to the exercise for assistance or to locate specific answers. Be prepared to submit this summary/report to your instructor at the designated time.

1. Explain how a climograph is constructed.

   _____

   _____

   _____

2. In your own words, provide some key words to describe the characteristics of each of the following Köppen climate groups.

   A climates: _____

   _____

   B climates: _____

   _____

   C climates: _____

   _____

   D climates: _____

   _____

   E climates: _____

   _____

   H climates: _____

   _____

3. List the general location of each of the following Köppen climate groups.

   A climates: _____

   _____

B climates: _____

_____

C climates: _____

_____

D climates: _____

_____

E climates: _____

_____

H climates: _____

_____

4. Indicate by name the Köppen climate group best described by each of the following statements.

   Vast areas of northern coniferous forests: _____

   Smallest annual range of temperature: _____

   The highest annual precipitation: _____

   Mean temperature of the warmest month is below 10°C: _____

   The result of high elevation and mountain slope orientation: _____

   Potential evaporation exceeds precipitation: ___

   Very little change in the monthly precipitation and temperature throughout the year: _____

Caused by the subsidence of air beneath high pressure cells: _____

_____

5. Using the data in Table 6, classify each station according to the most appropriate Köppen climate group. Where in North America is each likely to be located?

Station 1: _____

_____

Station 2: _____

_____

Station 3: _____

_____

Table 6   **Climatic Data for Question 5**

	J	F	M	A	M	J	J	A	S	O	N	D	YEAR
Station 1													
Temp. (°C)	1.7	4.4	7.9	13.2	18.4	23.8	25.8	24.8	21.4	14.7	6.7	2.8	13.8
Precip. (mm)	10	10	13	13	20	15	30	32	23	18	10	13	207
Station 2													
Temp. (°C)	−10.4	−8.3	−4.6	3.4	9.4	12.8	16.6	14.9	10.8	5.5	−2.3	−6.4	3.5
Precip. (mm)	18	25	25	30	51	89	64	71	33	20	18	15	459
Station 3													
Temp. (°C)	10.2	10.8	13.7	17.9	22.2	25.7	26.7	26.5	24.2	19.0	13.3	10.0	18.4
Precip. (mm)	66	84	99	74	91	127	196	168	147	71	53	71	1247

8

Shaping Earth's Surface
Arid and Glacial Landscapes

You may already have studied the hydrologic cycle and the role of running water and groundwater in shaping the landscape in humid regions. However, when taken together, the dry regions of the world and those areas whose surfaces have been modified by glacial ice also comprise a significant portion of Earth's surface (Figure 1). Since desert or near-desert conditions and glaciated regions prevail over a large area of Earth, an understanding of the landforms and processes that shaped these regions is essential to the Earth scientist.

Objectives

After you have completed this exercise, you should be able to:

1. Locate the desert and steppe regions of North America.
2. Describe the evolution of the landforms that exist in the mountainous desert areas of the Basin and Range region of the western United States.
3. Describe the different types of glacial deposits and the features they compose.
4. Identify and explain the formation of the features commonly found in areas where the landforms are the result of deposition by continental ice sheets.
5. Describe the evolution and appearance of a glaciated mountainous area.
6. Identify and explain the formation of the features caused by alpine glaciation.

Materials

calculator   ruler   hand lens

Materials Supplied by Your Instructor

stereoscope   string

Terms

desert	bajada	till
steppe	playa lake	stratified drift
flash flood	inselberg	moraine
Basin and Range	pediment	Pleistocene epoch
fault-block	alpine glacier	arête
mountains	continental ice	cirque
alluvial fan	sheet	horn
	drift	hanging valley

Figure 1 Glacial striations in bedrock, Yellowknife, Canada NWT. (Photo courtesy of Dr. Richard Waller, Keele University, UK)

Desert Landscapes

Arid **(desert)** and semiarid **(steppe)** climates cover about 30 percent of Earth's land area (Figure 2). At first glance, many desert landscapes with their angular hills and steep canyon walls may appear to have been shaped by processes other than those that are responsible for landforms in regions with an abundance of water. However, as striking as the contrasts may be, running water is still the dominant agent responsible for most of the erosional work in deserts. Wind erosion, although more significant in dry areas than elsewhere, is only of secondary importance.

The distinct effects that running water has on humid and dry areas are the result of the same processes operating under different climatic conditions. Precipitation in the dry climates is minimal, often sporadic, and frequently comes in the form of torrential downpours that last only a short time. Consequently, in desert areas **flash floods** occur, and few streams or rivers reach the sea because the water often evaporates and infiltrates into the ground.

Evolution of a Mountainous Desert Landscape

Mountainous desert landscapes have developed in response to a variety of geologic processes. A classic region for studying the effects of running water in dry areas is the western United States. Throughout much of this **Basin and Range** region, which includes southeastern California, Nevada, western Utah, southern Oregon, southern Arizona and New Mexico, the erosion of mountain ranges and subsequent deposition of sediment in adjoining basins have produced a landscape characterized by several unique landforms (Figure 3).

In a large area of the Basin and Range region of the western United States **fault-block mountains** have formed as large blocks of Earth's crust have been forced upward (Figure 3A). The infrequent and intermittent precipitation in this desert region typically results in streams that carry their eroded material from the mountains into interior basins. **Alluvial fans** and **bajadas** often form as streams deposit sediment on the less steep slopes at the base of the mountains (Figure 3B). On rare occasions when streams flow across the alluvial fans, a shallow **playa lake** may develop near the center of a basin.

Continuing erosion in the mountains and deposition in the basins may eventually fill the basin and only isolated peaks, called **inselbergs**, surrounded by gently sloping sediment, remain. As the front of the mountain is worn back by erosion, a broad, sloping bedrock surface called a **pediment**, covered by a thin layer of sediment, often forms at its base (Figure 3C). In the final stages, even the inselbergs will disappear, and all that remains is a nearly flat, sediment-covered surface underlain by the erosional remnants of mountains.

Use Figure 2 to answer questions 1 and 2.

1. Where are the desert and steppe regions of North America located?

   Desert: _____

   Steppe: _____

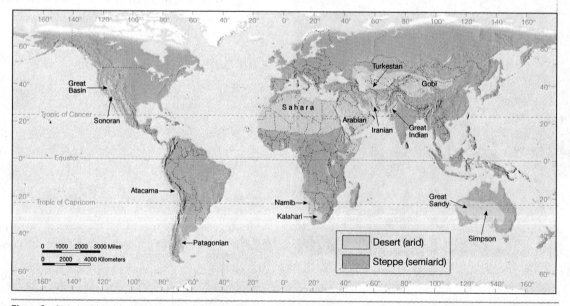

Figure 2 Global arid and semiarid climates cover about 30% of Earth's land surface. No other climate group covers so large an area. Low-latitude dry climates are the result of the global distribution of air pressure and winds. Middle-latitude deserts and steppes exist principally because they are sheltered in the deep interiors of large landmasses.

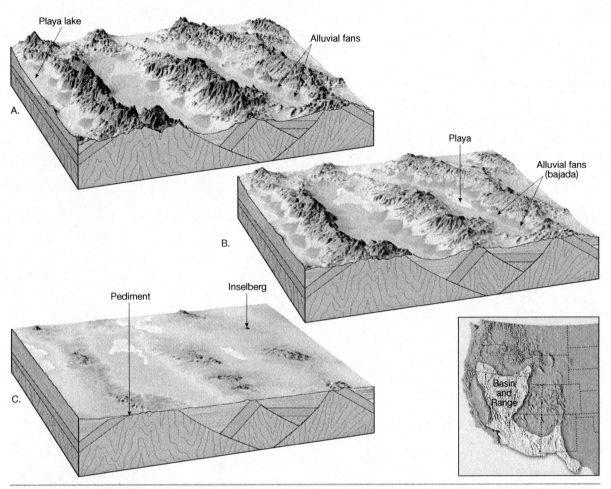

Figure 3   Stages of landscape evolution in a block-faulted, mountainous desert such as the Basin and Range region of the West. **A.** Early stage; **B.** Middle stage; **C.** Late stage.

2. Using an "X" to mark your selection(s), indicate which of the following statements are commonly held misconceptions concerning the world's dry lands.

   _____ The world's dry lands are always hot.

   _____ Desert landscapes are almost completely covered with sand dunes.

   _____ The dry regions of the world encompass about 30 percent of Earth's land surface.

   _____ Dry lands are practically all lifeless.

   Figure 4 is a portion of the Antelope Peak, Arizona, topographic map that illustrates many of the features of the mountainous desert landscapes found in the western United States. Use the map and accompanying stereogram of the area (Figure 5) to answer questions 3–13. You may find the diagrams in Figure 3 helpful.

3. On the map, outline the area that is illustrated in the stereogram.

   Use a stereoscope to examine the stereogram, Figure 5.

4. The vegetation in the area is (dense, sparse), and there are (few, many) dry stream courses. Circle your answers.

5. By examining the map, determine the total relief of the map area.

   Total relief = _____ ft

6. (Continuously flowing, Intermittent) streams dominate the area shown on the map. Circle your answer.

7. On the map, of the two lines, A or B (A, B), follows the steepest slope. Circle your answer.

8. By drawing arrows on the map, indicate the directions that intermittent streams will flow as they leave the mountains.

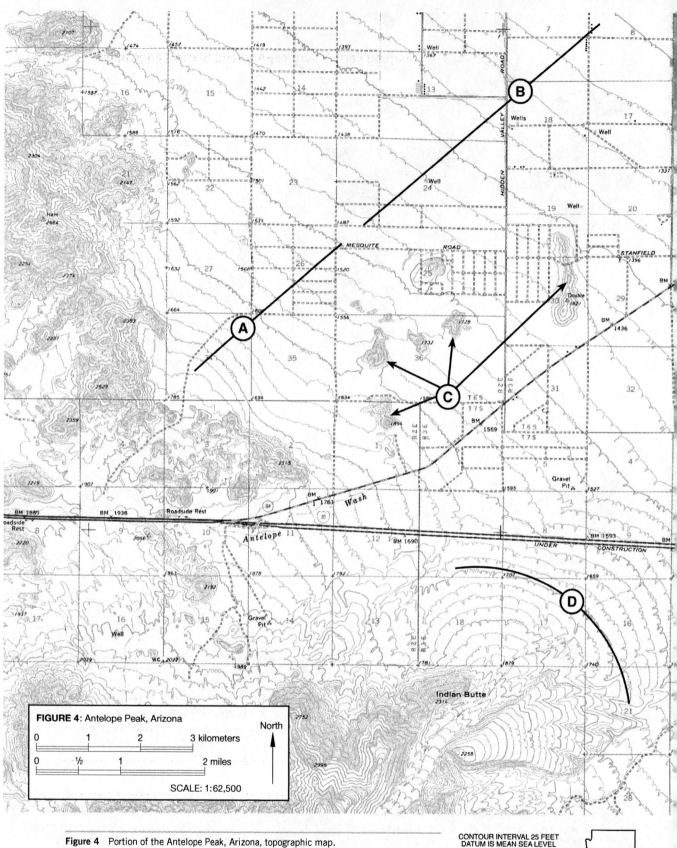

FIGURE 4: Antelope Peak, Arizona

| 0 | | 1 | | 2 | | 3 kilometers |

| 0 | ½ | | 1 | | | 2 miles |

SCALE: 1:62,500

North

Figure 4 Portion of the Antelope Peak, Arizona, topographic map.
(Map source: United States Department of the Interior, Geological Survey)

CONTOUR INTERVAL 25 FEET
DATUM IS MEAN SEA LEVEL

ARIZONA

QUADRANGLE LOCATION

104

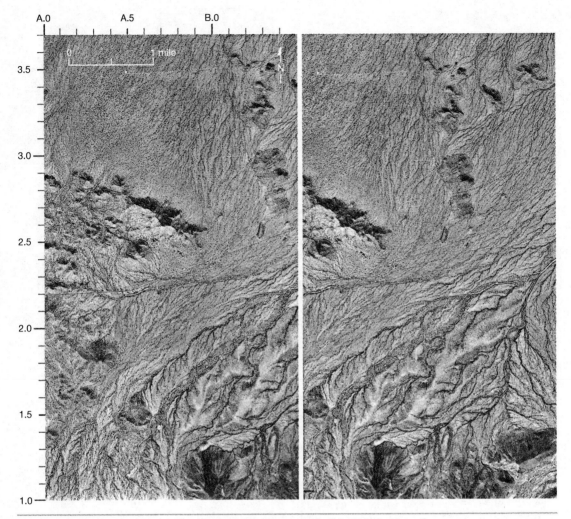

Figure 5   Stereogram of the Antelope Peak, Arizona, area. (Courtesy of the U.S. Geological Survey)

9. Where on the map is the most likely place that surface water may accumulate? Label the area "possible lake."

10. Identify the features indicated on the map at the following letters and briefly describe how each formed.

   Letter C: _____

   _____

   Letter D: _____

   _____

   The area at letter A on the map is a bedrock surface covered by a thin layer of sediment.

11. The feature labeled A is called a(n) _____.

12. Briefly describe how the Antelope Peak area may have looked millions of years ago.

   _____

   _____

   _____

13. Assume that erosion continues in the area without interruption. How might the area look millions of years from now?

   _____

   _____

   _____

Glacial Landscapes

Slightly more than 2% of the world's water is in the form of glacial ice that covers nearly 10% of Earth's land area. However, to an Earth scientist, glaciers represent more than storehouses of fresh water in the hydrologic cycle. Like the other agents that modify the surface, glaciers are dynamic forces capable of eroding, transporting, and depositing sediment.

Literally thousands of glaciers exist on Earth today. They occur in regions where, over long periods of time, the yearly snowfall has exceeded the quantity lost by melting or evaporation. **Alpine**, or **valley, glaciers** form from snow and ice at high altitudes. At high latitudes, enormous **continental ice sheets** cover much of Greenland and Antarctica.

Glacial erosion and deposition leave an unmistakable imprint on Earth's surface. In regions once covered by continental ice sheets, glacially scoured surfaces and subdued terrain dominated by glacial deposits are the rule (see Figure 1). By contrast, erosion by alpine glaciers in mountainous areas tends to accentuate the irregularity of the topography, often resulting in spectacular scenery characterized by sharp, angular features.

Glacial Deposits and Depositional Features

The general term **drift** applies to all sediments of glacial origin, no matter how, where, or in what form they were deposited. There are two types of glacial drift: (1) **till**, which is characteristically unsorted sediment deposited directly by the glacier (Figure 6), and (2) **stratified drift**, which is material that has been sorted and deposited by glacial meltwater.

The most widespread depositional features of glaciers are **moraines**, which are ridges of till that form along the edges of glaciers and layers of till that accumulate on the ground as the ice melts and recedes. There are several types of moraines, some common only to alpine glaciers, as well as other kinds of glacial depositional features.

Figure 7 illustrates a hypothetical retreating glacier. Use Figure 7 to answer questions 14–16.

14. Draw a large arrow on Figure 7 that indicates the direction of glacial ice movement in the area. Label the arrow "ice flow."

15. On Figure 7, label an example of a terminal moraine, recessional moraine, and ground moraine.

Features of Continental Ice Sheets

During a division of Earth's history called the **Pleistocene epoch**, continental ice sheets, as well as alpine glaciers, were considerably more extensive over Earth's surface than they are today. At one time, these thick sheets of ice covered all of Canada, portions of

Close up of cobble

Figure 6 Glacial till is an unsorted mixture of many different sediment sizes. A close examination often reveals cobbles that have been scratched as they were dragged along by the glacier. (Photos by E. J. Tarbuck)

Alaska, and much of the northern United States as well as extensive areas of northern Europe and Asia (Figure 8). Today, the impact that these ice sheets had on the landscape is still very obvious.

Use Figure 8 as a reference to answer question 16.

16. By listing state abbreviations, indicate the geographic area of the continental United States that Pleistocene glaciers covered during their maximum extent.

_____

_____

While alpine glaciers change the shape of the land surface primarily by erosion, landforms produced by

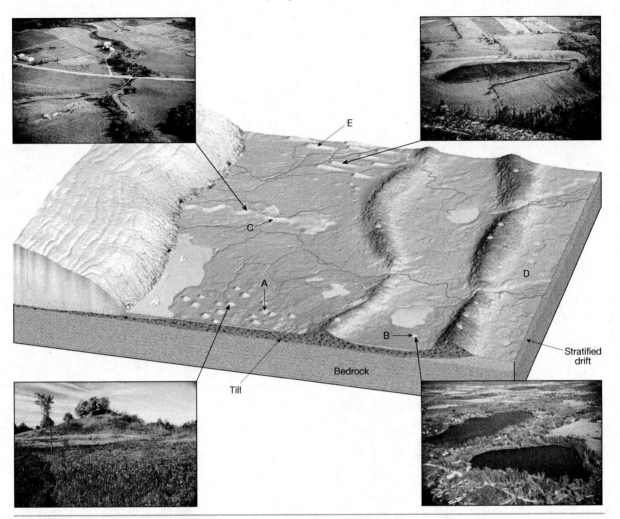

Figure 7   Characteristic depositional features of glaciers. (Drumlin photo courtesy of Ward's Natural Science Establishment; Kame, Esker, and Kettle photos by Richard P. Jacobs/JLM Visuals)

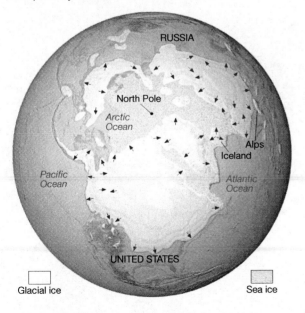

Figure 8   Maximum extent of glaciation in the Northern Hemisphere during the Pleistocene epoch.

Figure 9 Portion of the Whitewater, Wisconsin, topographic map. (Map source: United States Department of the Interior, Geological Survey)

FIGURE 9: Whitewater, Wisconsin

North

0   1   2   3 kilometers

0   ½   1   2 miles

SCALE: 1:62,500

CONTOUR INTER VAL 20 FEET
DOTTED LINES REPRESENT 10-FOOT CONTOURS
DATUM IS MEAN SEA LEVEL

WISCONSIN

continental ice sheets, especially those that covered portions of the United States during the Pleistocene epoch, are essentially depositional in origin. Some of the most extensive areas of glacial deposition occurred in the north-central United States. Here, glacial drift covers the surface and landscapes are dominated by moraines, outwash plains, kettles, and other depositional features.

17. Briefly describe each of the following glacial depositional features and select the letter on Figure 7 that indicates an example of each.

    Drumlin: _____

    _____ Letter: _____

    Esker: _____

    _____ Letter: _____

    Kame: _____

    _____ Letter: _____

    Kettle: _____

    _____ Letter: _____

Outwash plain: _____

_____ Letter: _____

Figure 9 is a portion of the Whitewater, Wisconsin, topographic map, which illustrates many of the depositional features that are typical of continental glaciation. Use the map and the accompanying stereogram of the area (Figure 10) to answer questions 18–30.

18. After examining the map and stereogram, draw a line on the map that outlines the area illustrated on the photograph.

19. The general topography of the land in the southeast quarter of the region is (higher, lower) in elevation and (more, less) irregular than the land in the northwest. Circle your answers.

20. What features on the map indicate that portions of the area are poorly drained? Where are these features located?

    _____

    _____

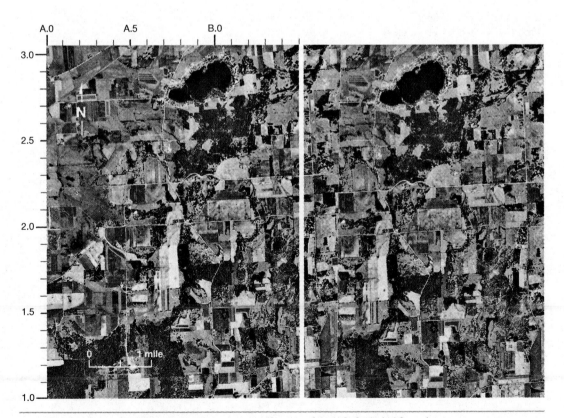

Figure 10   Stereogram of the Whitewater, Wisconsin, area. (Courtesy of the U.S. Geological Survey)

NORTHWEST   SOUTHEAST

Scuppernong River   Little Prairie

Figure 11   Northwest–southeast topographic profile of the Whitewater map.

Examine the elevations of the feature indicated with the letter As on the map that, in general, coincides with Kettle Moraine State Forest. Compare the elevations to those found to the northwest and southeast of the feature.

21. In Figure 11, sketch a northwest–southeast topographic profile along a line that extends from the Scuppernong River to near the city of Little Prairie. Indicate the appropriate elevations on the vertical axis of the profile.

22. The area that coincides with Kettle Moraine State Forest is (higher, lower) in elevation than the land to the northwest and southeast. Circle your answer.

23. The feature labeled with As on the map is a long ridge composed of till called a (kettle, moraine, drumlin). Circle your answer.

24. The streamlined, asymmetrical hills composed of till, labeled B, are what type of feature?

_____

25. Examine the shape of the features labeled B on the map and in Figure 7. How can the features be used to determine the direction of ice flow in a glaciated area?

_____

26. Use the features labeled B as a guide to draw an arrow on the map that indicates the direction of ice flow in the region.

27. Where on the map is the likely location of the outwash plain? Identify and label the area "outwash plain."

_____

28. Identify and label the ground moraine area on the map.

29. What term is applied to the numerous almost circular depressions designated with the letter Cs on the map?

_____

30. What is the probable origin of the material that is being mined in the gravel pits north and northeast of Palmyra?

_____

_____

_____

Features of Alpine or Valley Glaciation

As they flow, alpine glaciers often exaggerate the already irregular topography of a region by eroding the mountain slopes and deepening the valleys. Figure 12 illustrates the changes that a formerly unglaciated mountainous area (Figure 12A) experiences as the result of alpine glaciation. Many of the landforms produced by glacial erosion, such as **arête, cirques, horns,** and **hanging valleys** (Figure 13), are identified in Figure 12C.

Questions 31–33 refer to Figure 12.

31. How has glaciation changed the shape and depth of the main valley?

_____

_____

Prior to glaciation, tributary streams were adjusted to the depth of the main valley.

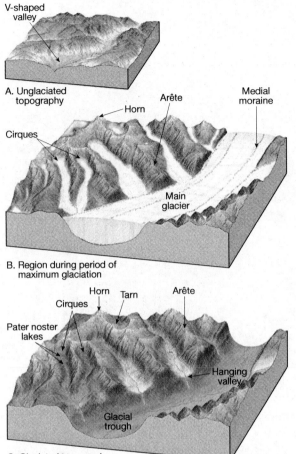

Figure 13 Bridalveil Falls in Yosemite National Park cascades from a hanging valley into the glacial trough below. (Photo by E. J. Tarbuck)

Figure 14 is an oblique aerial photograph of an area experiencing alpine glacial erosion on Mont Blanc, France. Questions 34 and 35 refer to the figure.

34. Draw arrows on the photograph that indicate the directions that the glaciers are flowing.

35. Give the name of the glacial feature described by each of the following statements as well as the letter on the photograph that labels an example of the feature. Use Figure 12C as a reference.

   a. Sinuous, sharp-edged ridge:

      Name: _____

      Letter of Example: _____

   b. Hollowed-out, bowl-shaped depression that is the glacier's source and the area of snow accumulation and ice formation:

      Name: _____

      Letter of Example: _____

   c. Moraine formed along the side of a valley:

      Name: _____

      Letter of Example: _____

   d. Moraine formed when two valley glaciers coalesce to form a single ice stream:

      Name: _____

      Letter of Example: _____

Figure 12 Landforms created by alpine glaciers. **A.** Landscape prior to glaciation; **B.** During glaciation; **C.** After glaciation.

32. What has been the consequence of glacial erosion on the gradients or slopes of tributary streams?

   _____

   _____

   _____

33. Use your own words to describe how the appearance of the area has changed from what it was prior to glaciation.

   _____

   _____

   _____

Figure 14 Oblique aerial photograph of alpine glaciers and glacial features, Mont Blanc, France. (Photo courtesy of U.S.G.S.)

Figure 15 is a portion of the Holy Cross, Colorado, topographic map, a mountainous area that underwent alpine glaciation in the past. Questions 36–41 refer to the map.

36. Following line A on the map, sketch a topographic profile of the valley of Lake Fork from Sugar Loaf Mtn. to Bear Lake on Figure 16. Indicate the appropriate elevations along the vertical axis of the profile.

37. Describe the shape of the profile of the valley of Lake Fork. The valley is called a glacial

_____

38. Identify the type of glacial feature indicated on the map at each of the following letters. Use Figure 12C as a reference.

Letter B: _____

Letter C: _____

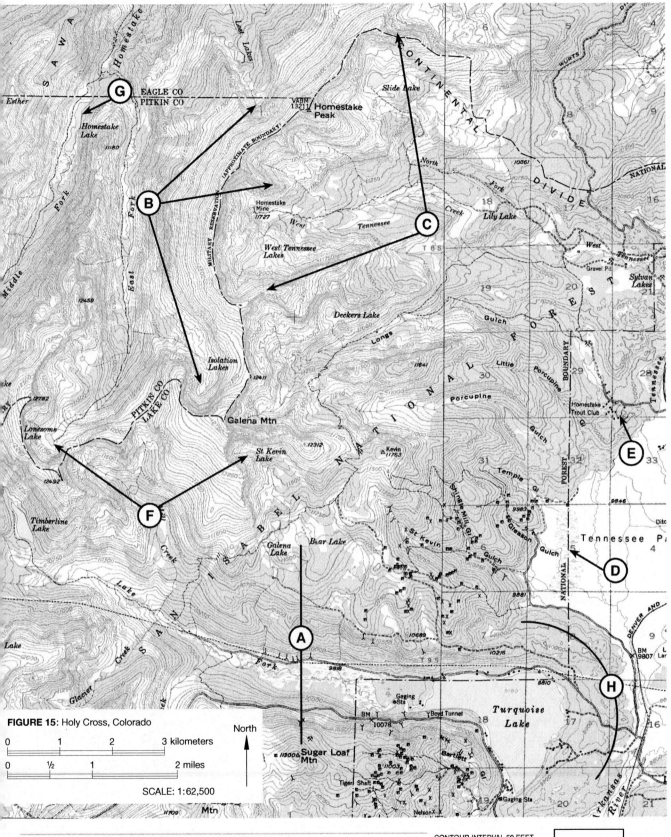

FIGURE 15: Holy Cross, Colorado

0   1   2   3 kilometers

0   ½   1   2 miles

SCALE: 1:62,500

North

Figure 15   Portion of the Holy Cross, Colorado, topographic map. (Map source: United States Department of the Interior, Geological Survey)

CONTOUR INTERVAL 50 FEET
DATUM IS MEAN SEA LEVEL

COLORADO

QUADRANGLE LOCATION

113

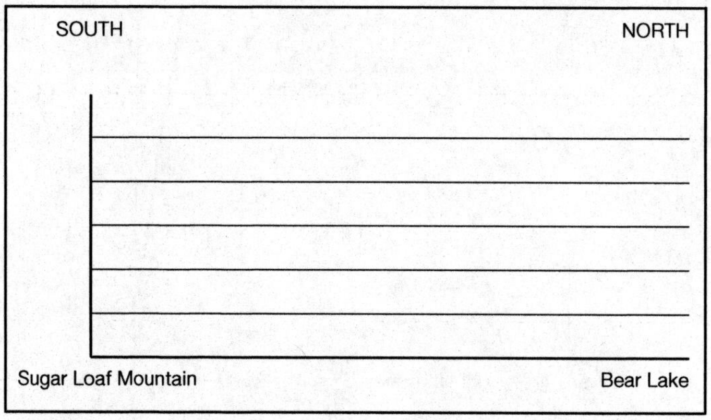

Figure 16 Topographic profile of the valley of Lake Fork on the Holy Cross map.

39. Letter (D, E, F, G) on the map indicates a *tarn*(s), a lake that forms in a cirque. Circle your answer.

The feature marked H on the map is composed of glacial till.

40. What type of glacial feature is designated H? How did it form?

_____

_____

41. What is the reason for the formation of Turquoise Lake?

_____

_____

Desert and Glaciers on the Internet

Investigate both desert and glacial regions by completing the corresponding online activity on the *Applications & Investigations in Earth Science* website at http://prenhall.com/earthsciencelab

Shaping Earth's Surface
Arid and Glacial Landscapes

Date Due: _____

Name: _____

Date: _____

Class: _____

After you have finished this exercise, complete the following questions. You may have to refer to the exercise for assistance or to locate specific answers. Be prepared to submit this summary/report to your instructor at the designated time.

1. What area of the United States is characterized by fault-block mountains with interior drainage into adjoining basins?

   _____

2. Describe the sequence of geologic events that have produced the landforms in the Antelope Peak area of Arizona.

   _____

   _____

3. What type of feature is located at each of the following letters on the Antelope Peak, Arizona, topographic map, Figure 4?

   Letter C: _____

   Letter D: _____

4. Toward what direction does the pediment slope on the Antelope Peak, Arizona, topographic map?

   _____

5. What is the reason for so many dry stream channels in the Antelope Peak, Arizona, area?

   _____

6. If you were working in the field, explain how you might determine whether a glacial feature is a recessional moraine or an esker.

   _____

   _____

   _____

   _____

   _____

7. In the following space, sketch a map-view (the area viewed from above) of the Whitewater, Wisconsin, topographic map, Figure 9. Show and label the outwash plain, end moraine, area containing drumlins, and the area containing kettles and kettle lakes.

115

8. Assume you are hiking in the mountains. You suspect that the area was glaciated in the past. Describe some of the features you would look for to confirm your suspicion.

_____

_____

9. What was your conclusion as to the reason for the formation of Turquoise Lake on the Holy Cross, Colorado, topographic map, Figure 15?

_____

10. On Figure 17, identify and label the alpine glacial features.

Figure 17   Athabaska Glacier in Canada's Jasper National Park. (Photo by David Barnes/The Stock Market)

9

EXERCISE

Shaping Earth's Surface
Running Water and Groundwater

The study of the processes that modify Earth's surface is of major significance to the Earth scientist. By understanding those processes and the features they produce, scientists gain insights into the geologic history of an area and make predictions concerning its future development.

Some of the agents that are responsible for modifying the surface of Earth are running water (Figure 1), groundwater, glacial ice, wind, and volcanic activity. Each produces a unique landscape with characteristic features that can be recognized on topographic maps. This exercise examines several of these agents, the variety of landforms associated with them, and some of the consequences of human interaction with these natural systems.

Objectives

After you have completed this exercise, you should be able to:

1. Sketch, label, and discuss the complete hydrologic cycle.

2. Explain the relation between infiltration and runoff that occurs during a rainfall.

3. Discuss the effect that urbanization has on the runoff and infiltration of an area.

4. Identify on a topographic map the following features that are associated with rivers and valleys: rapids, meanders, floodplain, oxbow lake, and backswamps.

5. Explain the occurrence, fluctuation, use, and misuse of groundwater supplies.

6. Identify on a topographic map the following features associated with karst landscapes: sinkholes, disappearing streams, and solution valleys.

Materials

calculator   hand lens
ruler
Materials Supplied by Your Instructor
graduated measuring   coarse sand, fine sand,
  cylinder (100 ml)   soil

Figure 1   Mountain stream. (Photo by E.J. Tarbuck)

small funnel   stereoscope
cotton   string
beaker (100 ml)

Terms

hydrologic cycle	permeability	aquifer
infiltration	hydrograph	karst topography
groundwater	discharge	disappearing
runoff	base level	stream
erosion	meander belt	solution valley
evaporation	zone of saturation	sinkhole
transpiration	water table	cave
porosity	zone of aeration	cavern

Introduction

On Earth, the water is constantly being exchanged between the surface and atmosphere. The **hydrologic cycle**, illustrated in Figure 2, describes this continuous movement of water from the oceans to the atmosphere, from the atmosphere to the land, and from the land back to the sea.

A portion of the precipitation that falls on land will soak into the ground via **infiltration** and become **groundwater**. If the rate of rainfall is greater than the surface's ability to absorb it, the additional water flows over the surface and becomes **runoff**. Runoff initially flows in broad sheets; however, it soon becomes confined and is channeled to form streams and rivers. **Erosion** by both groundwater and runoff wears down the land and modifies the shape of Earth's surface. Eventually runoff and groundwater from the continents return to the sea or the atmosphere, continuing the endless cycle.

Examining the Hydrologic Cycle

Figure 2 illustrates Earth's water balance, a quantitative view of the hydrologic cycle. Although the figure correctly implies a uniform exchange of water between Earth's atmosphere and surface on a worldwide basis, factors such as climate, soil type, vegetation, and urbanization often produce local variations.

Use Figure 2 as a reference to answer questions 1–6.

1. On a worldwide basis, more water is evaporated into the atmosphere from the (oceans, land). Circle your answer.

2. Approximately what percent of the total water evaporated into the atmosphere comes from the oceans?

$$\text{Percent from oceans} = \frac{\text{ocean evaporation}}{\text{total evaporation}} \times 100$$

= _____ %

Notice in the figure that more water evaporates from the oceans than is returned directly to them by precipitation.

3. Since sea level is not dropping, what are the other sources of water for the oceans in addition to precipitation?

_____

Over most of Earth, the quantity of precipitation that falls on the land must eventually be accounted for by the sum total of **evaporation**, **transpiration** (the release of water vapor by vegetation), **runoff**, and **infiltration**.

4. Define each of the following four variables.

Evaporation: _____

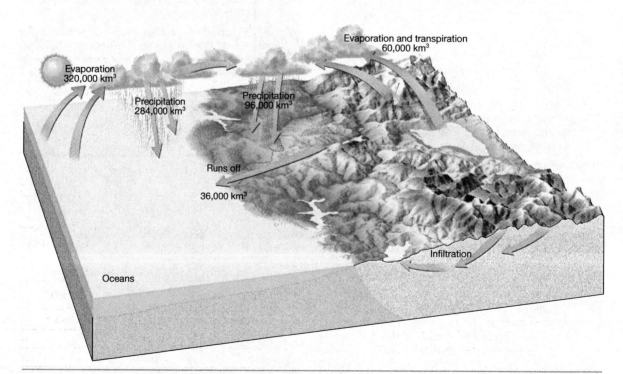

Figure 2   Earth's water balance, a quantitative view of the hydrologic cycle.

Transpiration: _____

Runoff: _____

Infiltration: _____

5. On a worldwide basis, about (35, 55, 75) percent of the precipitation that falls on the land becomes runoff. Circle your answer.

6. At high elevations or high latitudes, some of the water that falls on the land does not immediately soak in, run off, evaporate, or transpire. Where is this water being temporarily stored?

_____

_____

Infiltration and Runoff

During a rainfall most of the water that reaches the land surface will infiltrate or run off. The balance between infiltration and runoff is influenced by factors such as the **porosity** and **permeability** of the surface material, slope of the land, intensity of the rainfall, and type and amount of vegetation. After infiltration saturates the land and the ground contains all the water it can hold, runoff will begin to occur on the surface.   -

7. Describe the difference between the terms *porosity* and *permeability*. Is it possible for a substance to have a high porosity and a low permeability? Why?

_____

_____

_____

_____

Permeability Experiment

To gain a better understanding of how the permeability of various Earth materials affects the flow of groundwater, examine the equipment setup in Figure 3 and conduct the following experiment by completing each of the indicated steps.

Step 1. Obtain the following equipment and materials from your instructor:
    graduated measuring cylinder
    beaker
    small funnel
    piece of cotton
    samples of coarse sand, fine sand, and soil (enough of each to fill the funnel approximately two-thirds full)

Step 2. Place a small wad of cotton in the neck of the funnel.

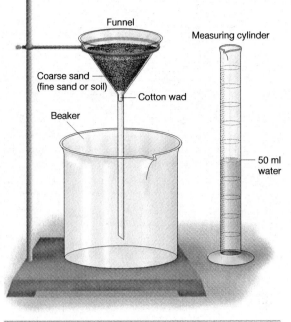

Figure 3 Equipment setup for permeability experiment.

Step 3. Fill the funnel above the cotton about two-thirds full with coarse sand.

Step 4. With the bottom of the funnel placed in the beaker, measure the length of time that it takes for 50 ml of water to drain through the funnel filled with coarse sand. Record the time in the data table, Table 1.

Step 5. Using the measuring cylinder, measure the amount (in milliliters) of water that has drained into the beaker and record the measurement in the data table.

Step 6. Empty and clean the measuring cylinder, funnel, and beaker.

Step 7. Repeat the experiment two additional times, using fine sand and then soil. Record the results of each experiment at the appropriate place in the data table, Table 1. (*Note:* In each case, fill the funnel with the material to the same level that was used for the coarse sand and use the same size wad of cotton.)

Step 8. Clean the glassware and return it to your instructor, along with any unused sand and soil.

Table 1   Data Table for Permeability Experiment

	Length of time to drain 50 ml of water through funnel	Milliliters of water drained into beaker
Coarse sand	seconds	ml
Fine sand	seconds	ml
Soil	seconds	ml

8. Questions 8a–8c refer to the permeability experiment.

   a. Of the three materials you tested, the (coarse sand, fine sand, soil) has the greatest permeability. Circle your answer.

   b. Suggest a reason why different amounts of water were recovered in the beaker for each material that was tested.

   _____

   c. Write a brief statement summarizing the results of your permeability experiment.

   _____

   _____

   _____

9. What will be the effect of each of the following conditions on the relation between infiltration and runoff?

   Highly permeable surface material: _____

   _____

   Steep slope: _____

   _____

   Gentle rainfall: _____

   _____

   Dense ground vegetation: _____

   _____

10. What will be the relation between infiltration and runoff in a region with a moderate slope that has a permeable surface material covered with sparse vegetation?

    _____

    _____

Infiltration and Runoff in Urban Areas

In urban areas much of the land surface has been covered with buildings, concrete, and asphalt. The consequence of covering large areas with impervious materials is to alter the relation between runoff and infiltration of the region.

Figure 4 shows two hypothetical **hydrographs** (plots of stream flow, or runoff, over time) for an area before and after urbanization. The amount of precipitation the area receives is the same after urbanization as before. Runoff is evaluated by measuring the stream **discharge**, which is the volume of water flowing past a given point per unit of time, usually measured in cubic feet per second. Use Figure 4 to answer questions 11–14.

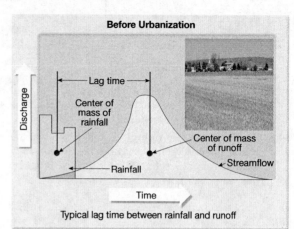

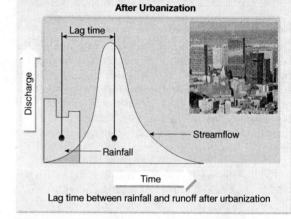

Figure 4 The effect of urbanization on stream flow before urbanization (top) and after urbanization (bottom). (After L. B. Leopold, U.S. Geological Survey Circular 559, 1968)

11. As illustrated in Figure 4, urbanization (increases, decreases) the peak, or maximum, stream flow. Circle your answer.

12. What is the effect that urbanization has on the lag time between the time of the rainfall and the time of peak stream discharge?

    _____

13. Total runoff occurs over a (longer, shorter) period of time in an area that has been urbanized. Circle your answer.

14. Based on what you have learned from the hydrographs, explain why urban areas often experience flash-flooding during intense rainfalls.

    _____

    _____

    _____

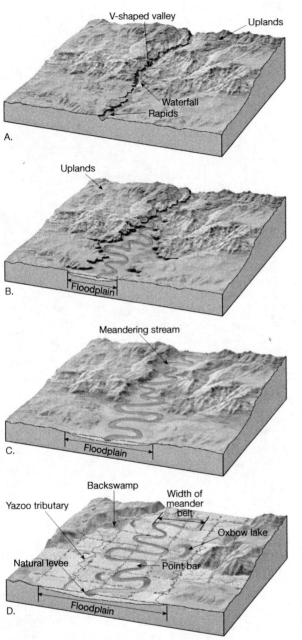

Figure 5 Common features of valleys. **A.** Near the headwaters.
B. and **C.** In the middle. **D.** At the mouth. (After Ward's Natural
Science Establishment, Inc., Rochester, New York)

Running Water

Of all the agents that shape Earth's surface, running
water is the most important. Rivers and streams are responsible for producing a vast array of erosional and
depositional landforms in both humid and arid regions. As illustrated in Figure 5, many of these features
are associated with the *headwaters* of a river, while others typically are found near the *mouth*.

An important factor that governs the flow of a
river is its **base level**. Base level is the lowest point to
which a river or stream may erode. The ultimate base
level is sea level. However, lakes, resistant rocks, and
main rivers often act as temporary, or local, base levels
that control the erosional and depositional activities of
a river for a period of time.

Often the *head*, or source area, of a river is well
above base level. At the headwaters, rivers typically
have steep slopes and downcutting prevails. As the
river deepens its valley it may encounter rocks that are
resistant to erosion and form *rapids* and *waterfalls*. In
arid areas rivers often erode narrow valleys with nearly vertical walls. In humid regions the effect of mass
wasting and slope erosion caused by heavy rainfall
produce typical V-shaped valleys (Figure 5A).

In humid regions downstream from the headwaters, the gradient or slope of a river decreases while its
discharge increases because of the additional water
being added by tributaries. As the level of the channel
begins to approach base level, the river's energy is directed from side to side and the channel begins to follow a sinuous path, or *meanders* (Figure 6). Lateral
erosion by the meandering river widens the valley
floor and a *floodplain* begins to form (Figures 5B and
5C).

Near the mouth of a river where the channel is
nearly at base level, maximum discharge occurs and
meandering often becomes very pronounced. Widespread lateral erosion by the meandering river produces a floodplain that is often several times wider
than the river's *meander belt*. Features such as *oxbow
lakes, natural levees, backswamps* or *marshes,* and *yazoo
tributaries* commonly develop on broad floodplains
(Figure 5D).

Figure 6 This high-attitude image shows incised meanders of the
Delores River in western Colorado. (Courtesy of USDA–ASCS)

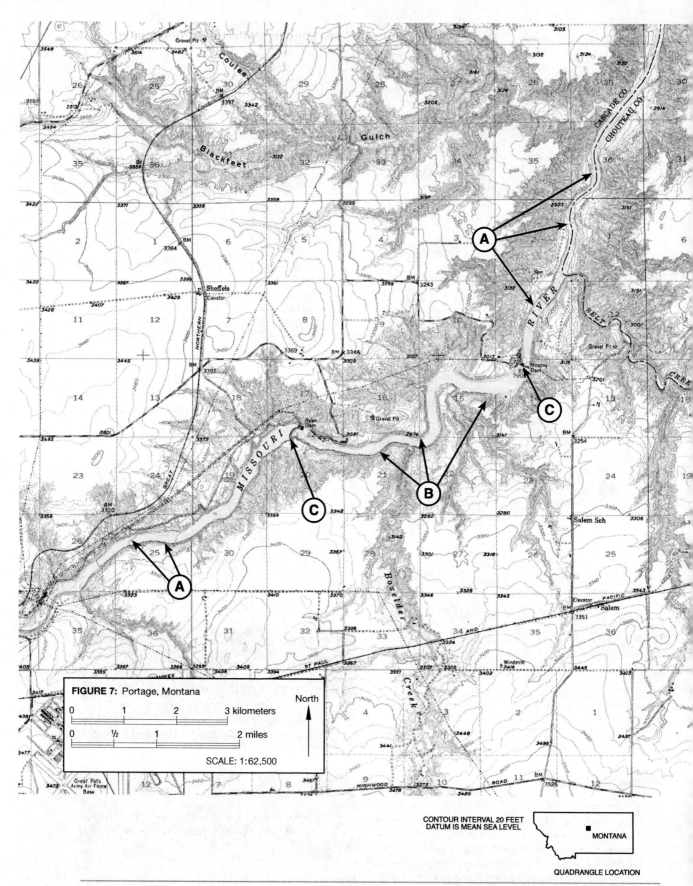

Figure 7 Portion of the Portage, Montana, topographic map. (Map source: United States Department of the Interior, Geological Survey)

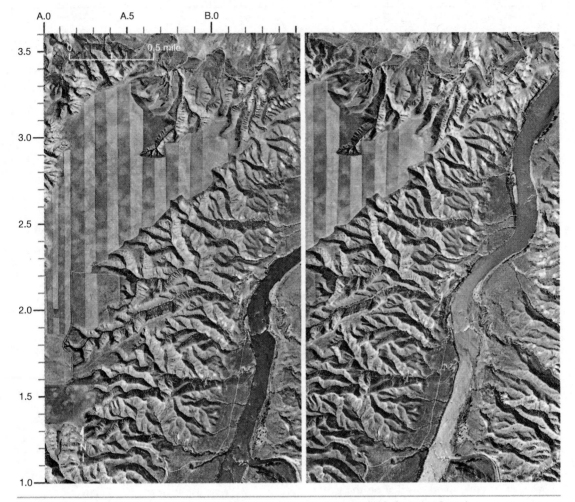

Figure 8   Stereogram of the Missouri River, vicinity of Portage, Montana. (Courtesy of U.S. Geological Survey)

Questions 15–25 refer to the Portage, Montana, topographic map, Figure 7, and stereogram of a portion of the same region, Figure 8. On the map, notice the rapids indicated by A and the steep-sided valley walls of the Missouri River indicated by B.

15. Compare the aerial photograph to the map. Then, on the topographic map, outline the area that is shown in the photo.

16. Use the map to determine the approximate total *relief* (vertical distance between the lowest and highest points of the area represented).

    Highest elevation (_____ ft) – lowest elevation (_____ ft) = total relief (_____ ft).

17. On Figure 9, draw a north–south topographic profile through the center of the map along a line from north of Blackfeet Gulch to south of the Missouri River. Indicate the appropriate elevations on the vertical axis of the profile. Label

Blackfeet Gulch and the Missouri River on the profile.

18. Label the upland areas between stream valleys on the topographic profile in Figure 9 with the word "upland."

19. The upland areas are (broad and flat, narrow ridges). Circle your answer.

20. Approximately what percentage of the area shown on the map is stream valley and what percentage upland?

    Stream valley: _____ %

    Upland: _____ %

21. Approximately how deep would the Missouri River have to erode to reach ultimate base level?

    _____ ft

NORTH   SOUTH

Figure 9 North–south topographic profile through the center of the Portage, Montana, map.

22. It appears that the Missouri River and its tributaries are, for the most part, actively (eroding, depositing) in the area. Circle your answer.

23. With increasing time, as the tributaries erode and lengthen their courses near the headwaters, what will happen to the upland areas?

_____

_____

Notice the dams located along the Missouri River at C.

24. What effect have the dams had on the width of the river, upriver from their locations?

_____

_____

25. Assuming that climate, base level, and other factors remain unchanged, how might the area look millions of years from now?

_____

_____

Questions 26–31 refer to the Angelica, New York, topographic map, Figure 10.

26. What is the approximate total relief shown on the map?

_____ feet of total relief

27. Draw an arrow on the map indicating the direction that the main river, the Genesee, is flowing. (*Hint:* Use the elevations of the contour lines on the floodplain to determine your answer.)

28. What is the approximate *gradient* (the slope of a river; generally measured in feet per mile) of the Genesee River?

Average gradient = _____ ft/mile

29. The Genesee River (follows a straight course, meanders from valley wall to valley wall). Circle your answer.

30. Most of the areas separating the valleys on the Angelica map are (very broad and flat, relatively narrow ridges). Circle your answer.

31. Assume that erosion continues in the region without interruption. How might the appearance of the area change over a span of millions of years?

_____

_____

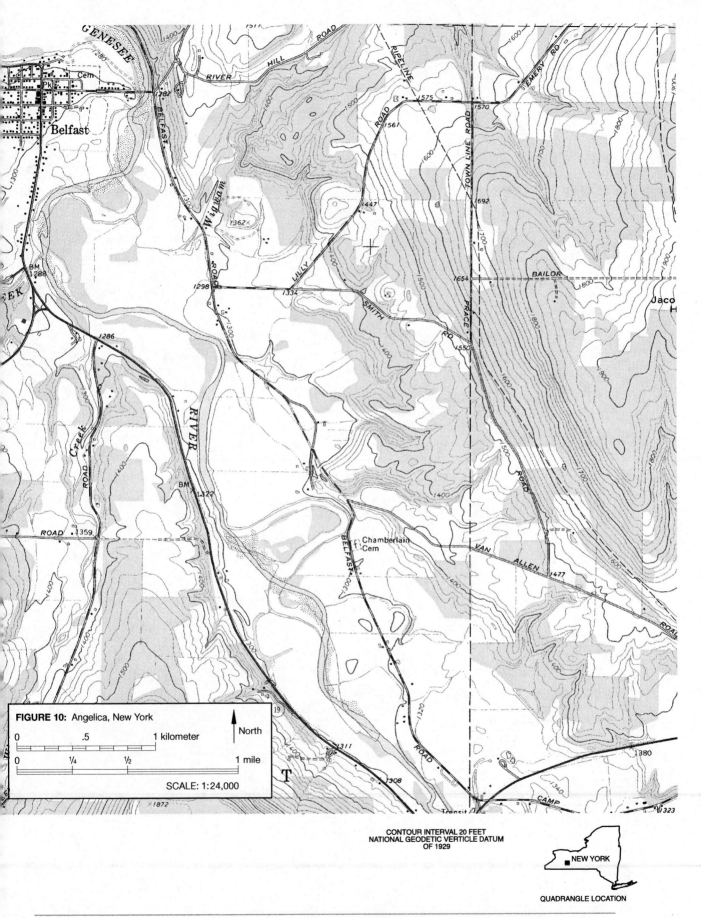

FIGURE 10: Angelica, New York

0   .5   1 kilometer

↑ North

0   ¼   ½   1 mile

SCALE: 1:24,000

CONTOUR INTERVAL 20 FEET
NATIONAL GEODETIC VERTICLE DATUM
OF 1929

NEW YORK

QUADRANGLE LOCATION

Figure 10   Portion of the Angelica, New York, topographic map. (Map source: United States Department of the Interior, Geological Survey)

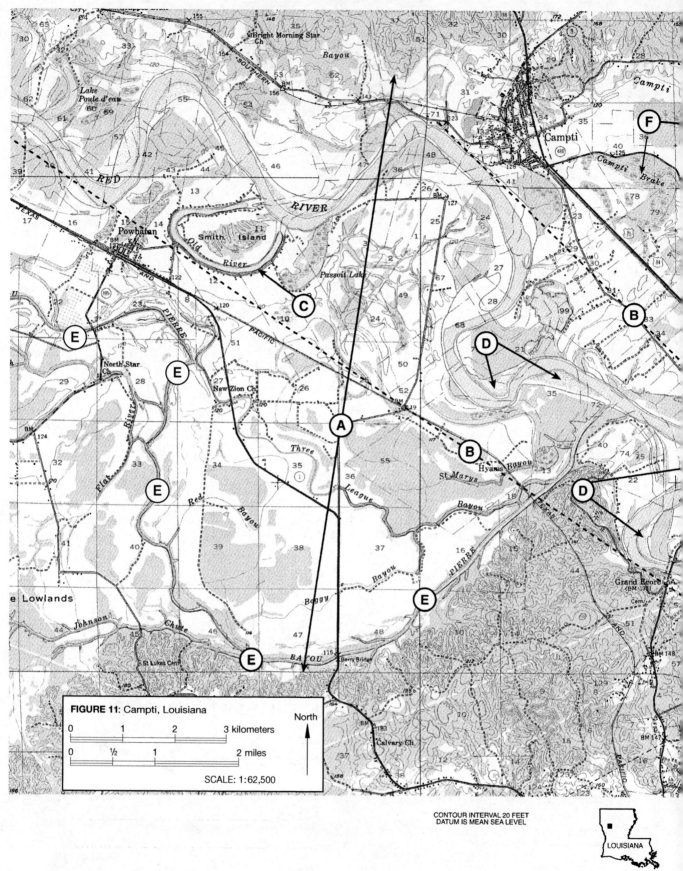

FIGURE 11: Campti, Louisiana

0   1   2   3 kilometers

0   ½   1   2 miles

SCALE: 1:62,500

North

CONTOUR INTERVAL 20 FEET
DATUM IS MEAN SEA LEVEL

LOUISIANA

QUADRANGLE LOCATION

Figure 11   Portion of the Campti, Louisiana, topographic map. (Map source: United States Department of the Interior, Geological Survey)

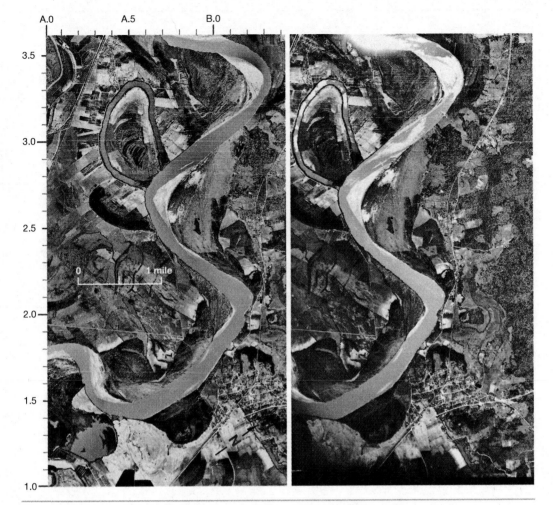

Figure 12   Stereogram of the Campti, Louisiana, area. (Courtesy of U.S. Geological Survey)

Questions 32–39 refer to the Campti, Louisiana, topographic map, Figure 11, and stereogram of the same area, Figure 12. On the map, A indicates the width of the floodplain of the Red River and the dashed lines, B, mark the two sides of the meander belt of the river.

32. Approximately what percentage of the map area is floodplain?

Floodplain = _____ % of the map area

33. In Figure 13, draw a north–south topographic profile along a line from the south edge of the City of Campti to south of Bayou Pierre. Indicate the appropriate elevations on the vertical axis of the profile. Label the floodplain area and Bayou Pierre on the sketch.

34. Approximately how many feet is the floodplain above ultimate base level?

_____ feet above ultimate base level

35. Using Figure 5 as a reference, identify the type of feature found at each of the following lettered positions on the map. Also, write a brief statement describing how each feature forms.

Letter C (in particular, *Old River*): _____

_____

Letter D: _____

_____

Letter E: _____

_____

Letter F: _____

_____

Figure 13   North–south topographic profile of the Campti map.

36. Identify and label examples of a point bar, cut-bank, and an oxbow lake on the stereogram.

37. Write a statement that compares the width of the meander belt of the Red River to the width of its floodplain.

_____

_____

38. (Downcutting, Lateral erosion) is the dominant activity of the Red River. Circle your answer.

39. Assuming that erosion by the Red River continues without interruption, what will eventually happen to the width of its floodplain?

_____

_____

_____

Answer questions 40–42 by comparing the Portage, Angelica, and Campti topographic maps.

40. On which of the three maps is the gradient of the main river the steepest?

_____

41. Which of the three areas has the greatest total relief (vertical distance between the lowest and highest elevations)?

_____

42. Choosing from the three topographic maps, write the name of the map that is best described by each of the following statements.

Primarily floodplain: _____

_____

River valleys separated by broad, relatively flat upland areas: _____

_____

Most of the area consists of steep slopes:

_____

Greatest number of streams and tributaries:

_____

Poorly drained lowland area with marshes and swamps: _____

_____

Active downcutting by rivers and streams:

_____

Surface nearest to base level: _____

_____

Groundwater

As a resource, groundwater supplies much of our water needs for consumption, irrigation, and industry. On the other hand, as a hazard, groundwater can damage building foundations and aid the movement of materials during landslides and mudflows. In many areas, overuse and contamination of this valuable resource threaten the supply. One of the most serious problems faced by many localities is land subsidence caused by groundwater withdrawal.

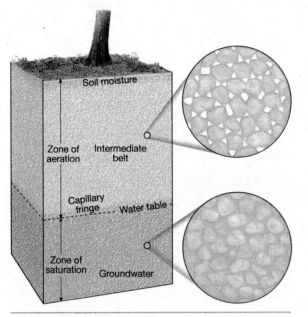

Figure 14   Idealized distribution of groundwater.

Water Beneath the Surface

Groundwater is water that has soaked into Earth's surface and occupies all the pore spaces in the soil and bedrock in a zone called the **zone of saturation**. The upper surface of this saturated zone is called the **water table**. Above the water table in the **zone of aeration**, the pore spaces of the materials are unsaturated and mainly filled with air. (Figure 14)

Figure 15 illustrates a profile through the subsurface of a hypothetical area. Use Figures 14 and 15 to answer questions 43–50.

43. Label the zone of saturation, zone of aeration, and water table on Figure 15.

44. Describe the shape of the water table in relation to the shape of the land surface.

_____

45. What is the relation of the surface of the water in the stream to the water table?

_____

46. What is the lowered surface in the water table around the well called? What has caused the lowering of the surface of the water table around the well? What will make it larger or smaller?

_____

_____

_____

47. At point *A* on Figure 15, sketch a small, impermeable pocket of clay that intersects the valley wall.

48. Describe what will happen to water that infiltrates to the depth of the clay pocket at point *A*.

_____

_____

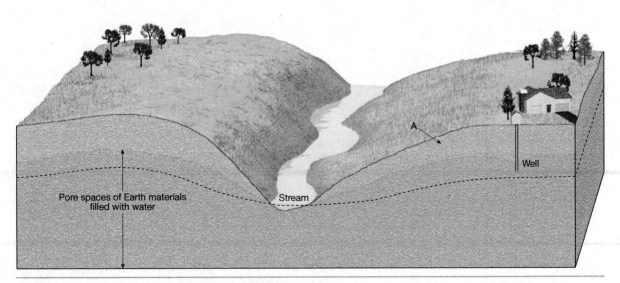

Figure 15   Earth's subsurface showing saturated and unsaturated materials.

Figure 16 Hypothetical topographic map showing the location of several water walls.

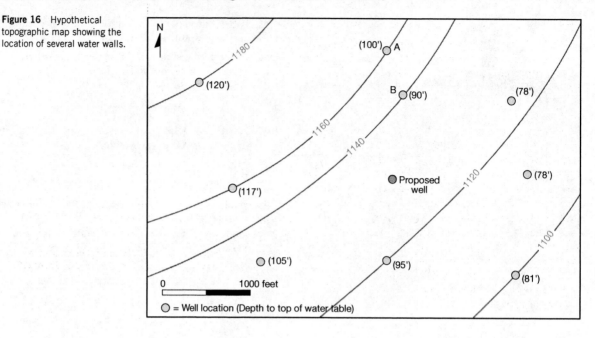

The dashed line in Figure 15 represents the level of the water table during the dry season when infiltration is no longer replenishing the groundwater.

49. What is the consequence of the lower elevation of the water table during the dry season on the operation of the well? How might the problem have been avoided?

_____

_____

50. What are two main sources of pollutants that can contaminate groundwater supplies?

_____

_____

Groundwater Movement

Figure 16 is a hypothetical topographic map showing the location of several water wells. The numbers in parentheses indicate the depth of the water table below the surface in each well.

Questions 51–53 refer to Figure 16.

51. Begin by calculating the elevation of the water table at each indicated well location. Then, using a colored pencil, draw smooth 10-foot contours that illustrate the slope of the water table in the area. Using a different colored pencil, draw arrow(s) on

the map that indicate the direction of the slope of the water table.

a. What is the average amount of slope of the water table in the area? Toward which direction does the water table slope?

_____

_____

b. Referring to the site of the proposed water well, at approximately what depth below the surface should the well drill the water table?

_____

52. Assume that a dye was put into well A at 1 PM on May 10, 1990, and detected in well B at 8 AM on October 1, 1998. What was the velocity of the groundwater movement between the two wells in centimeters per day?

_____

_____

53. Use a different colored pencil to draw dashed 10-ft contour lines on the map that illustrate the configuration of the water table after well B was pumped for a sufficient period of time to lower the water table 22 feet at its location. Assume that an area within a 500-foot radius of well B was affected by the pumping.

The Problem of Ground Subsidence

As the demand for freshwater increases, surface subsidence caused by the withdrawal of groundwater from **aquifers** presents a serious problem for many areas. Several major urban areas such as Las Vegas, Houston-Galveston, Mexico City, and the Central Valley of California are experiencing subsidence caused by over-pumping wells (Figure 17). In Mexico City alone, compaction of the subsurface material resulting from the reduction of fluid pressure as the water table is lowered has caused as much as seven meters of subsidence. Fortunately, in many areas an increased reliance on surface water and replenishing the groundwater supply has slowed the trend.

A classic example of land subsidence caused from groundwater withdrawal is in the Santa Clara Valley, which borders the southern part of San Francisco Bay in California. The graph presented in Figure 18 illustrates the relation between ground subsidence in the valley and the level of water in a well in the same area.

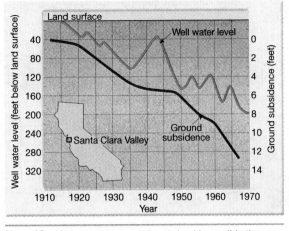

Figure 18   Ground subsidence and water level in a well in the Santa Clara Valley, California. (Data courtesy of U.S. Geological Survey)

Figure 17   The marks on this utility pole indicate the level of the surrounding land in preceding years. Between 1925 and 1977 this part of the San Joaquin Valley, CA subsided almost 9 meters because of the withdrawal of groundwater and the resulting compaction of sediments. (Photo courtesy of U.S. Geological Survey)

Questions 54–58 refer to Figure 18.

54. What is the general relation between the ground subsidence and level of water in the well illustrated on the graph?

_____

_____

55. What was the total ground subsidence and total drop in the level of water in the well during the period shown on the graph?

    Total ground subsidence = _____ ft

    Total drop in well level = _____ ft

56. During the period shown on the graph, on an average, about (1 ft, 5 ft, 10 ft) of land subsidence occurred with each 20-ft decrease in the level of water in the well. Circle your answer.

57. The ground subsidence that took place during the twenty years before 1950 was (less, greater) than the subsidence that took place between 1950 and 1970. Circle your answer.

58. Notice that minimal subsidence took place between 1935 and 1950. After referring to the well water level during the same period of time, suggest a possible reason for the reduced rate of subsidence between 1935 and 1950.

_____

_____

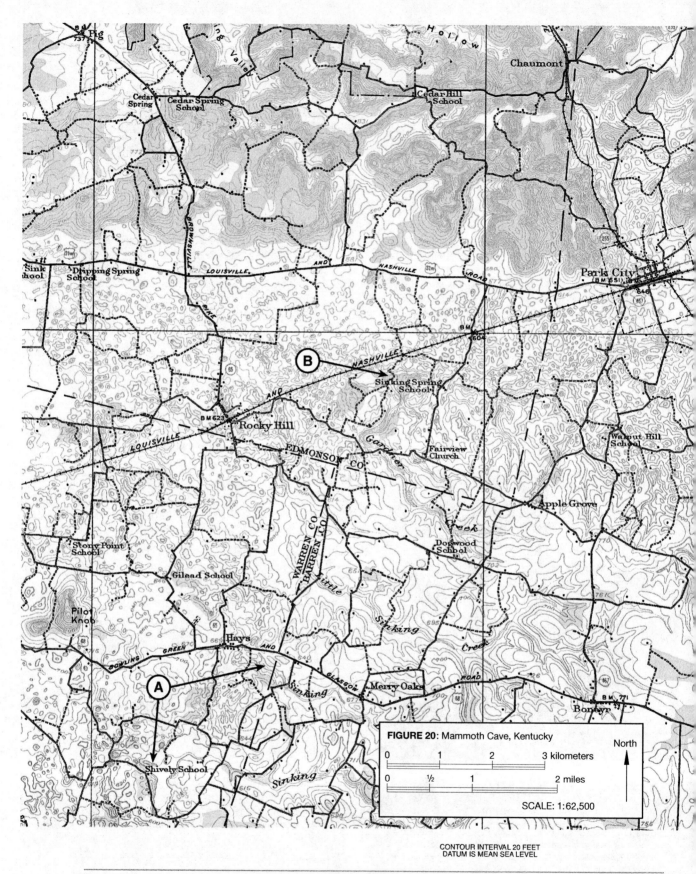

Figure 20 Portion of the Mammoth Cave, Kentucky, topographic map. (Map source: United States Department of the Interior, Geological Survey)

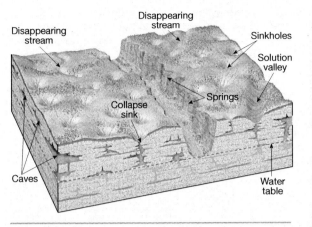

Figure 19   Generalized features of an advanced stage of karst topography.

Examining a Karst Landscape

Landscapes that are dominated by features that form from groundwater dissolving the underlying rock are said to exhibit **karst topography** (Figure 19). On the surface, karst topography is characterized by irregular terrain, springs, **disappearing streams**, **solution valleys**, and depressions called **sinkholes** (Figure 19). Beneath the surface, dissolution of soluble rock may result in **caves** and **caverns**.

One of the classic karst regions in the United States is the Mammoth Cave, Kentucky, area. Locate and examine the Mammoth Cave, Kentucky, topographic map, Figure 20. An insoluble sandstone layer is the surface rock that forms the upland area in the northern quarter of the map. Underneath the sandstone layer is a soluble limestone. Erosion has removed all the sandstone in the southern three fourths of the map and exposed the limestone. On the limestone surface, numerous sinkholes, indicated by closed contour lines with hachures, are present, as well as several disappearing streams (letter A).

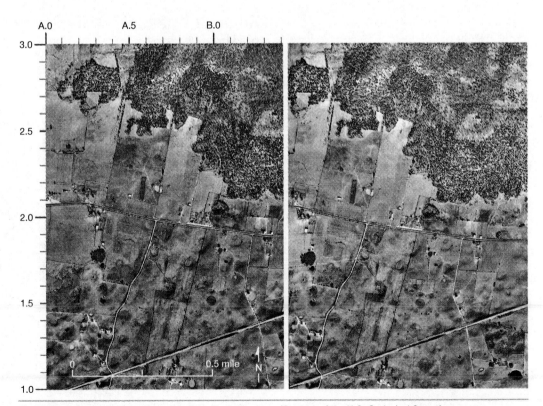

Figure 21   Stereogram of the Mammoth Cave, Kentucky, area. (Courtesy of the U.S. Geological Survey)

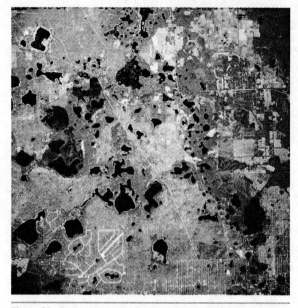

Figure 22   This high-altitude infrared image shows an area of karst topography in central Florida. The numerous lakes occupy sinkholes. (Courtesy of USDA–ASCS)

Use the Mammoth Cave topographic map, Figure 20, the stereogram of the same area, Figure 21, and Figure 22 to answer questions 59–63.

59. On the topographic map, outline the area that is shown on the stereogram.

60. What does the absence of water in the majority of sinkholes indicate about the depth of the water table in the area?

_____

61. Examine both the stereogram and map. Then describe the difference in appearance between the northern quarter and southern three-fourths of the mapped area.

_____

_____

_____

_____

62. Describe what is happening to Gardner Creek in the area indicated with the letter B on the map.

_____

63. List two ways that sinkholes commonly form.

a. _____

b. _____

Running Water and Groundwater on the Internet

Apply the concepts from this exercise to investigate the hydrology of a river and the groundwater resources in your home state by completing the corresponding online activity on the *Applications & Investigations in Earth Science* website at http://prenhall.com/earthsciencelab

Shaping Earth's Surface
Running Water and Groundwater

Date Due: _____

Name: _____

Date: _____

Class: _____

After you have finished this exercise, complete the following questions. You may have to refer to the exercise for assistance or to locate specific answers. Be prepared to submit this summary/report to your instructor at the designated time.

1. Write a statement that describes the movement of water through the hydrologic cycle, citing several of the processes that are involved.

   _____

   _____

   _____

Figure 23 River and valley features. (Photo by Michael Collier)

2. Assume you are assigned a project to determine the quantity of infiltration that takes place in an area. What are the variables you must measure or know before you can arrive at your answer?

   _____

   _____

3. Write a brief paragraph summarizing the results of your permeability experiment in question 8 of the exercise.

   _____

   _____

   _____

4. Describe the effects that urbanization has on the stream flow of a region.

   _____

5. On Figure 23, identify and label as many features of the river and valley as possible. Write a brief paragraph describing the area and its relation to base level.

   _____

   _____

   _____

   _____

   _____

135

6. Refer to the proportion of water that either infiltrates or runs off. Why does a soil-covered hillside with sparse vegetation often experience severe soil erosion? What are some soil conservation methods that could be used to reduce the erosion?

_____

_____

_____

7. Name and describe two features you would expect to find on the floodplain of a widely meandering river near its mouth.

Feature   Description

_____   _____

_____   _____

8. Assume you have decided to drill a water well. What are at least two factors concerning the water table and zone of saturation that should be considered prior to drilling?

_____

_____

9. What is the average slope of the water table illustrated on Figure 16?

_____

10. What was the velocity of the groundwater movement between wells A and B in Figure 16?

_____

11. How might a rapidly growing urban area that relies on groundwater as a freshwater source avoid the problem of land subsidence from groundwater withdrawal?

_____

_____

12. Name and describe two features you would expect to find in a region with karst topography.

Feature   Description

_____   _____

_____   _____

10

EXERCISE

Earthquakes and Earth's Interior

Almost all of Earth lies beneath us, yet its accessibility to direct examination is limited. Therefore, one of the most difficult problems faced by Earth scientists is determining the physical properties of Earth's interior. The branch of Earth science called **seismology** combines mathematics and physics to explain the nature of earthquakes and how they can be used to gather information about Earth beyond our view. This exercise introduces some of the techniques that are used by seismologists to determine the location of an earthquake and to investigate the structure of Earth's interior.

Objectives

After you have completed this exercise, you should be able to:

1. Examine an earthquake seismogram and recognize the P waves, S waves, and surface waves.

2. Use a seismogram and travel-time graph to determine how far a seismic station is from the epicenter of an earthquake.

3. Determine the actual time that an earthquake occurred using a seismogram and travel-time graph.

4. Locate the epicenter of an earthquake by plotting seismic data from three seismic stations.

5. Explain how earthquakes are used to determine the structure of Earth's interior.

6. List the name, depth, composition, and state of matter of each of Earth's interior zones.

7. Describe the temperature gradient of the upper Earth.

8. Explain why Earth scientists think that the asthenosphere consists of partly melted, plastic material at a depth of about 100 kilometers.

9. Explain how earthquakes and Earth's temperature gradient have been used to explain the fact that large, rigid slabs of the lithosphere are descending into the mantle at various locations on Earth.

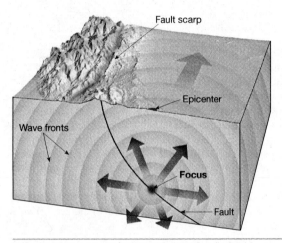

Figure 1 Earthquake focus and epicenter. The focus is the zone within Earth where the initial displacement occurs. The epicenter is the surface location directly above the focus.

Materials

calculator   colored pencils
drawing compass   ruler

Materials Supplied by Your Instructor

atlas or wall map

Terms

seismology   P wave   asthenosphere
lithosphere   S wave   mantle
focus   surface wave   outer core
seismic wave   amplitude   inner core
seismograph   period   geothermal gradient
seismogram   epicenter

From *Applications and Investigations in Earth Science,* Sixth Edition, Edward J. Tarbuck, Frederick K. Lutgens, Kenneth G. Pinzke. Copyright © 2009 by Pearson Education, Inc. Published by Pearson Prentice Hall. All rights reserved.

Earthquakes

Earthquakes are vibrations of Earth that occur when the rigid materials of the **lithosphere** are strained beyond their limit, yield, and "spring back" to their original shape, rapidly releasing stored energy. This energy radiates in all directions from the source of the earthquake, called the **focus**, in the form of **seismic waves**. (Figure 1). **Seismograph** instruments (Figure 2) located throughout the world amplify and record the ground motions produced by passing seismic waves on **seismograms** (Figure 3). The seismograms are then used to determine the time of occurrence and location of an earthquake, as well as to define the internal structure of Earth.

Examining Seismograms

The three basic types of seismic waves generated by an earthquake at its focus are **P waves**, **S waves**, and **surface waves** (Figure 4). P and S waves travel through Earth while surface waves are transmitted along the outer layer. Of the three wave types, P waves have the greatest velocity and, therefore, reach the seismograph station first. Surface waves arrive at the seismograph station last. P waves also have smaller **amplitudes** (range from the mean, or average, to the extreme) (Figure 3) and shorter **periods** (time interval between the arrival of successive wave crests) than S and surface waves.

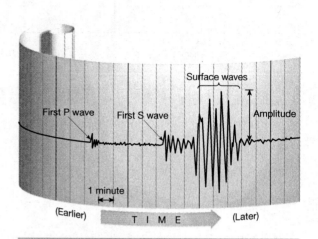

Figure 3 Typical earthquake seismogram.

On Figure 3, a typical earthquake recording on a seismogram, each vertical line marks a one-minute time interval. Answer questions 1–6 by referring to Figure 3.

1. It took approximately (5, 7, 11) minutes to record the entire earthquake from the first recording of the P waves to the end of the surface waves. Circle your answer.

2. (Five, Seven) minutes elapsed between the arrival of the first P wave and the arrival of the first S wave on the seismogram. Circle your answer.

3. (Five, Seven) minutes elapsed between the arrival of the first P wave and the first surface wave.

4. The maximum amplitude of the surface waves is approximately (5, 9) times greater than the maximum amplitude of the P waves.

5. The approximate period of the surface waves is (10, 30, 60) seconds.

6. The period of the surface waves is (greater, less) than the period for P waves.

Locating an Earthquake

The focus of an earthquake is the actual place within Earth where the earthquake originates. Earthquake foci have been recorded to depths as great as 600 km. When locating an earthquake on a map, seismologists plot the **epicenter**, the point on Earth's surface directly above the focus (Figure 1).

The difference in the velocities of P and S waves provides a method for locating the epicenter of an earthquake. Both P and S waves leave the earthquake focus at the same instant. Since the P wave has a greater velocity, the further away the recording instrument is from the focus, the greater will be the difference in the arrival times of the first P wave compared to the first S wave.

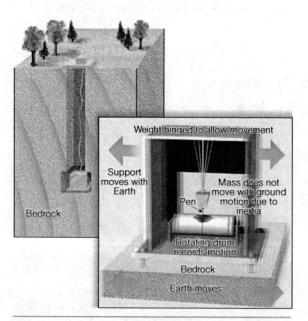

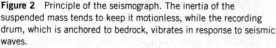

Figure 2 Principle of the seismograph. The inertia of the suspended mass tends to keep it motionless, while the recording drum, which is anchored to bedrock, vibrates in response to seismic waves.

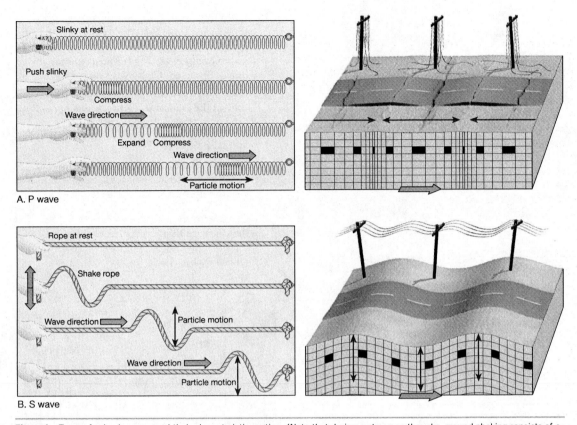

A. P wave

B. S wave

Figure 4 Types of seismic waves and their characteristic motion. (Note that during a strong earthquake, ground shaking consists of a combination of various kinds of seismic waves.) **A.** As illustrated by a slinky, P waves are compressional waves that alternately compress and expand the material through which they pass. The back-and-forth motion produced as compressional waves travel along the surface can cause the ground to buckle and fracture, and may cause power lines to break **B.** S waves cause material to oscillate at right angles to the direction of wave motion. Because S waves can travel in any plane, they produce up-and-down and sideways shaking of the ground.

To determine the distance between a recording station and an earthquake epicenter, find the place on the travel-time graph, Figure 5, where the vertical separation between the P and S curves is equal to the number of minutes difference in the arrival times between the first P and first S waves on the seismogram. From this position, a vertical line is drawn that extends to the top or bottom of the graph and the distance to the epicenter is read.

To accurately locate an earthquake epicenter, records from three different seismograph stations are needed. First, the distance that each station is from the epicenter is determined using Figure 5. Then, for each station, a circle centered on the station with a radius equal to the station's distance from the epicenter is drawn. The geographic point where all three circles, one for each station, intersect is the earthquake epicenter (Figure 6).

Answering questions 7–16 will help you understand the process used to determine an earthquake epicenter.

7. An examination of Figure 5 shows that the difference in the arrival times of the first P and the first

S waves on a seismogram (increases, decreases), the farther a station is from the epicenter. Circle your answer.

8. Use Figure 5 to determine the difference in arrival times (in minutes) between the first P wave and first S wave for stations that are the following distances from an epicenter.

1,000 miles: _____ minutes difference

2,400 km: _____ minutes difference

3,000 miles: _____ minutes difference

On the seismogram in Figure 3, you determined the difference in the arrival times between the first P and the first S waves to be five minutes.

9. Refer to the travel-time graph. What is the distance from the epicenter to the station that recorded the earthquake in Figure 3?

_____ miles

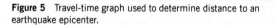

Figure 5 Travel-time graph used to determine distance to an earthquake epicenter.

10. From the travel-time (minutes) axis of the travel-time graph, the first P waves from the seismogram in Figure 3 arrived at the recording station approximately (3, 7, 14) minutes after the earthquake occurred. Circle your answer.

11. If the first P wave was recorded at 10:39 P.M. local time at the station in Figure 3, what was the local time when the earthquake actually occurred?

_____ P.M. local time

Figure 7 illustrates seismograms for the same earthquake recorded at New York, Seattle, and Mexico City. Use this information to answer questions 12–16.

12. Use the travel-time graph, Figure 5, to determine the distance that each station in Figure 7 is from the epicenter. Write your answers in the epicenter data table, Table 1.

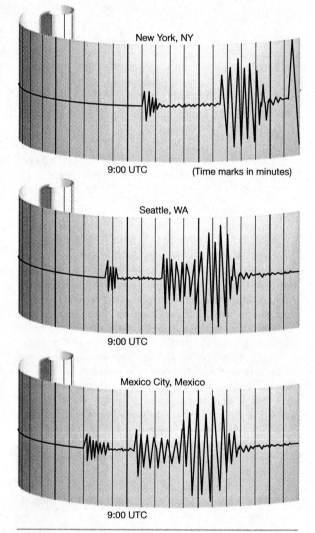

Figure 7 Three seismograms of the same earthquake recorded at three different locations.

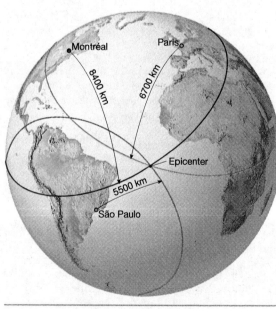

Figure 6 An earthquake epicenter is located using the distances obtained from three or more seismic stations.

Table 1 Epicenter Data Table

	NEW YORK	SEATTLE	MEXICO CITY
Elapsed time between first P and first S waves			
Distance from epicenter in miles			

13. After referring to an atlas or wall map, accurately place a small dot showing the location of each of the three stations on the map provided in Figure 8. Also label each of the three cities.

14. On Figure 8, use a drawing compass to draw a circle around each of the three stations with a radius, in miles, equal to its distance from the epicenter. (*Note:* Use the distance scale provided on the map to set the distance on the drawing compass for each station.)

15. What is the approximate latitude and longitude of the epicenter of the earthquake that was recorded by the three stations?

    _____ latitude and _____ longitude

16. Note on the seismograms that the first P wave was recorded in New York at 9:01 Coordinated Universal Time (UTC, the international standard on which most nations base their civil time). At what time (UTC) did the earthquake actually occur?

    _____ UTC

Global Distribution of Earthquakes

Earth scientists have determined that the global distribution of earthquakes is not random but follows a few relatively narrow belts that wind around Earth. Figure 9 illustrates the world distribution of earthquakes for a period of several years. Use the figure to answer questions 17 and 18.

17. With what Earth feature is each of the following earthquake belts associated?

    Western and southern Pacific Ocean basin: _____

    _____

    Western South America: _____

    _____

    Mid-Atlantic Ocean basin: _____

    _____

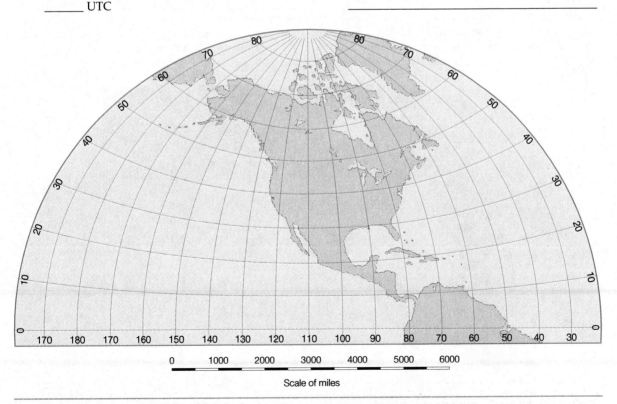

Figure 8 Map for locating an earthquake epicenter.

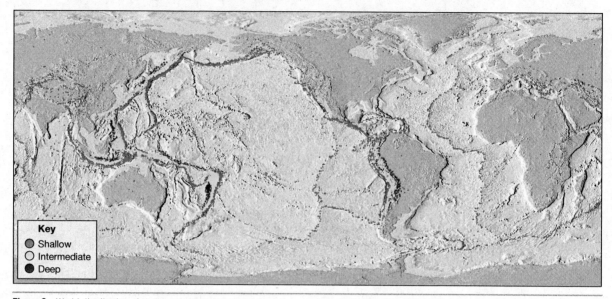

Figure 9   World distribution of shallow-, intermediate-, and deep-focus earthquakes. (Data from NOAA)

18. The belts of earthquake activity follow closely the boundaries of what Earth phenomenon?

The Earth Beyond Our View

The study of earthquakes has contributed greatly to Earth scientists' understanding of the internal structure of Earth. Variations in the travel times of P and S waves as they journey through Earth provide scientists with an indication of changes in rock properties. Also, since S waves cannot travel through fluids, the fact that they are not present in seismic waves that penetrate deep into Earth suggests a fluid zone near Earth's center.

In addition to the lithosphere, the other major zones of Earth's interior include the **asthenosphere**, **mantle**, **outer core**, and **inner core**. After you have reviewed these zones and the general structure of the Earth's interior, use Figure 10 to answer questions 19–24.

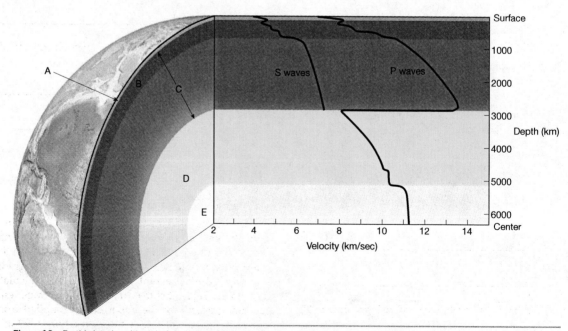

Figure 10   Earth's interior with variations in P and S wave velocities. (Data from Bruce A. Bolt)

19. The layer labeled A on Figure 10 is the solid, rigid, upper zone of Earth that extends from the surface to a depth of about (100, 500, 1,000) kilometers. Circle your answer.

    a. Zone A is called the (core, mantle, lithosphere).

    b. What are the approximate velocities of P and S waves in zone A?

       P wave velocity: _____ km/sec

       S wave velocity: _____ km/sec

    c. The velocity of both P and S waves (increases, decreases) with increased depth in zone A. Circle your answer.

    d. List the two parts of Earth's *crust* that are included in zone A and briefly describe the composition of each.

       1) _____: _____

       _____

       2) _____: _____

       _____

20. Zone B is the part of Earth's upper mantle that extends from the base of zone A to a depth of up to about (180, 660, 2,250) kilometers in some regions of Earth. Circle your answer.

    a. Zone B is called the (crust, asthenosphere, core).

    b. The velocity of P and S waves (increases, decreases) immediately below zone A in the upper part of zone B.

    c. The change in velocity of the S waves in zone B indicates that it (is, is not) similar to zone A.

21. Zone C (which includes the lower part of zone A and zone B) extends to a depth of

    _____ kilometers.

    a. Zone C is called Earth's _____.

    b. What fact concerning S waves indicates that zone C is not liquid?

       _____

       _____

    c. What is the probable composition of zone C?

       _____

22. Zone D extends from 2,885 km to about (5,100, 6,100) kilometers.

    a. Zone D is Earth's _____ _____.

    b. What happens to S waves when they reach zone D, and what does this indicate about the zone?

       _____

       _____

       _____

       _____

    c. The velocity of P waves (increases, decreases) as they enter zone D. Circle your answer.

23. Zone E is Earth's _____ _____.

    a. Zone E extends from a depth of _____ km to the _____ of Earth.

    b. What change in velocity do P waves exhibit at the top of zone E, and what does this suggest about the zone?

       _____

       _____

       _____

       _____

    c. What is the probable composition of Earth's core?

       _____

       _____

24. Label Figure 10 by writing the name of each interior zone at the appropriate letter.

Earth's Internal Temperature

Measurements of temperatures in wells and mines have shown that Earth's temperatures increase with depth. The rate of temperature increase is called the **geothermal gradient.** Although the geothermal gradient varies from place to place, it is possible to calculate an average. Table 2 shows an idealized average temperature gradient for the upper Earth compiled from many different sources. Use the information in Table 2 to answer questions 25–29.

Table 2 Idealized Internal Temperatures of Earth Compiled from Several Sources

DEPTH (KILOMETERS)	TEMPERATURE (°C)
0	20°
25	600°
50	1000°
75	1250°
100	1400°
150	1700°
200	1800°

Table 3 Melting Temperatures of Granite (with water) and Basalt at Various Depths within Earth

GRANITE (WITH WATER)		BASALT	
DEPTH (KM)	MELTING TEMP. (°C)	DEPTH (KM)	MELTING TEMP. (°C)
0	950°	0	1100°
5	700°	25	1160°
10	660°	50	1250°
20	625°	100	1400°
40	600°	150	1600°

25. Plot the temperature values from Table 2 on the graph in Figure 11. Then draw a single line that fits the pattern of points from the surface to 200 km. Label the line "temperature gradient."

26. Refer to the graph in Figure 11. The rate of increase of Earth's internal temperature (is constant, changes) with increasing depth. Circle your answer.

27. The rate of temperature increase from the surface to 100 km is (greater, less) than the rate of increase below 100 km.

28. The temperature at the base of the lithosphere, which is about 100 kilometers below the surface, is approximately (600, 1,400, 1,800) degrees Celsius.

29. Use the data and graph to calculate the average temperature gradient (temperature change per unit of depth) for the upper 100 km of Earth in °C/100 km and °C/km.

    °C/100 km: _____, °C/km: _____

Melting Temperatures of Rocks

Geologists have always been concerned with the conditions required for pockets of molten rock (magma) to form near the surface, as well as at what depth within

Earth a general melting of rock may occur. The melting temperature of a rock changes as pressure increases deeper within Earth. The approximate melting points of the igneous rocks, granite and basalt, under various pressures (depths) have been determined in the laboratory and are shown in Table 3. Granite and basalt have been selected because they are the common materials of the upper Earth. Use the data in Table 3 to answer questions 30–35.

30. Plot the melting temperature data from Table 3 on the Earth's internal temperature graph you have prepared in Figure 11. Draw a different colored line for each set of points and label them "melting curve for wet granite" and "melting curve for basalt."

    Use the graphs you have drawn in Figure 11 to help answer questions 31–33.

31. Assume your Earth temperature gradient is accurate. At approximately what depth within Earth would wet granite reach its melting temperature and form granitic magma?

    _____ km within Earth

32. Evidence suggests that the oceanic crust and the remaining lithosphere down to a depth of about 100 km are similar in composition to basalt. The melting curve for basalt indicates that the lithosphere above approximately 100 km (has, has not) reached the melting temperature for basalt and therefore should be (solid, molten). Circle your answers.

33. Figure 11 indicates that basalt reaches its melting temperature within Earth at a depth of approximately _____ km. (Solid, Partly melted) basaltic material would be expected to occur below this depth. Circle your answer.

34. Referring to Figure 10, what is the name of the zone within Earth that begins at a depth of about 100 km and may extend to approximately 700 km?

    _____

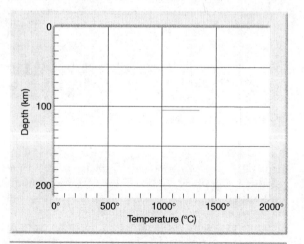

Figure 11 Graph for plotting temperature curves.

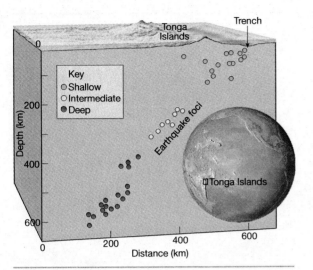

Figure 12   Distribution of earthquake foci in 1965 in the vicinity of the Tonga Islands. (Data from B. Isacks, J. Oliver, and L. R. Sykes)

35. Why do scientists believe that the zone in question 34 is capable of "flowing"?

_____

_____

Earthquakes and Earth Temperatures—A Practical Application

The study of earthquakes and Earth's internal temperature has contributed greatly to the understanding of plate tectonics. One part of the plate tectonics theory is that large, rigid slabs of the lithosphere are descending into the mantle where they generate deep focus earthquakes. Using earthquakes and Earth temperatures, Earth scientists have confirmed that this major Earth process is currently taking place near the Tonga Islands in the South Pacific and elsewhere.

Figure 12 illustrates the distribution of earthquake foci during a one-year period in the vicinity of the Tonga Islands. Use the figure to answer questions 36–40.

36. At approximately what depth do the deepest earthquakes occur in the area represented on Figure 12?

_____ kilometers

37. The earthquake foci in the area are distributed (in a random manner, nearly along a line). Circle your answer.

38. On the figure, outline the area of earthquakes within Earth.

39. Using previous information from this exercise, draw a line on Figure 12 at the proper depth that indicates the top of the *asthenosphere*—the zone of partly melted or plastic Earth material. Label the line "top of asthenosphere."

40. Recall the cause and mechanism of earthquakes. Why have Earth scientists been drawn to the conclusion of a descending slab of solid lithosphere being consumed into the mantle near Tonga?

_____

_____

_____

_____

Earthquakes on the Internet

Continue your exploration of earthquakes by completing the corresponding online activity on the *Applications & Investigations in Earth Science* website at http://prenhall.com/earthsciencelab

Notes and calculations.

Earthquakes and Earth's Interior

Date Due: _____

Name: _____

Date: _____

Class: _____

After you have finished this exercise, complete the following questions. You may have to refer to the exercise for assistance or to locate specific answers. Be prepared to submit this summary/report to your instructor at the designated time.

1. Use the minute marks provided below to sketch a typical seismogram where the first P wave arrives three minutes ahead of the first S wave. Label each type of wave.

. . . .

(minute marks)

2. How far from the earthquake epicenter is the seismic station that recorded the seismogram in question 1 of this Summary/Report page?

_____ miles

3. Use a diagram to explain how the epicenter of an earthquake is located.

Explanation: _____

_____

_____

_____

_____

_____

_____

Epicenter Diagram

4. What are three Earth features associated with earthquakes?

_____

_____

5. The change in velocity of S waves at the top of the asthenosphere suggests that it is (similar to, different from) the lithosphere. Circle your answer.

6. Why don't S waves make it through Earth's outer core?

_____

_____

_____

7. List the depths of the following interior zones of Earth.

Crust: depth (km) from _____ to _____

Mantle: depth (km) from _____ to _____

Outer core: depth (km) from _____ to _____

Inner core: depth (km) from _____ to _____

8. On the internal temperature graph you constructed in Figure 11, at what depth did you determine granitic magma should form?

_____ kilometers

9. Why do Earth scientists think that rigid slabs of the lithosphere are descending into the mantle near the Tonga Islands?

_____

_____

10. Define the following terms:

Earthquake focus: _____

_____

Earthquake epicenter: _____

_____

Seismogram: _____

_____

Asthenosphere: _____

_____

Geothermal gradient: _____

_____

Lithosphere: _____

_____

11. Identify, label, and describe each of Earth's interior zones on Figure 13.

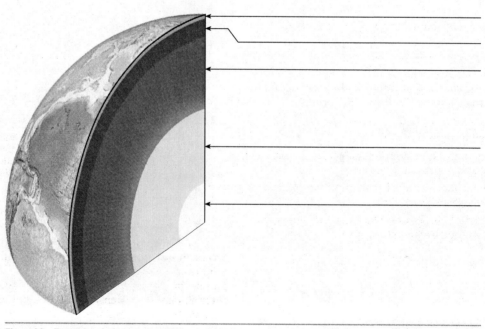

Figure 13 Earth's interior zones.

11

EXERCISE

Introduction to Oceanography

The global ocean covers nearly three quarters of Earth's surface and **oceanography** is an important focus of Earth science studies. This exercise investigates some of the physical characteristics of the oceans. To establish a foundation for reference, the extent, depths, and distribution of the world's oceans are the first topics examined. Salinity and temperature, two of the most important variables of seawater, are studied to ascertain how they influence the density of water and the deep ocean circulation (Figure 1).

Objectives

After you have completed this exercise, you should be able to:

1. Locate and name the major water bodies on Earth.
2. Discuss the distribution of land and water in each hemisphere.
3. Locate and describe the general features of ocean basins.
4. Explain the relation between salinity and the density of seawater.
5. Describe how seawater salinity varies with latitude and depth in the oceans.
6. Explain the relation between temperature and the density of seawater.
7. Describe how seawater temperature varies with latitude and depth in the oceans.

Materials

colored pencils   ruler

Materials Supplied by Your Instructor

measuring cylinder (100 ml, clear, Pyrex or plastic)	world wall map, globe, or atlas	test tubes
		dye
	ice	salt
salt solutions	beaker	rubber band

Figure 1 The deep-diving submersible *Alvin* is 7.6 meters long, weighs 16 tons, has a cruising speed of 1 knot, and can reach depths as great as 4000 meters. A pilot and two scientific observers are along during a normal 6- to 10-hour dive. (Courtesy of Rod Catanach/Woods Hole Oceanographic Institution)

Terms

oceanography	deep-ocean trench	submarine
continental shelf	mid-ocean ridge	canyons
continental slope	density	turbidity
abyssal plain	density current	currents
seamount	salinity	

Extent of the Oceans

1. Refer to a globe, wall map of the world, or world map in an atlas and identify each of the oceans

and major water bodies listed below. Locate and label each on the world map, Figure 2.

Oceans	Other Major Water Bodies	
A. Pacific	1. Caribbean Sea	11. Arabian
B. Atlantic	2. North Sea	Sea
C. Indian	3. Coral Sea	12. Weddell
D. Arctic	4. Sea of Japan	Sea
	5. Sea of Okhotsk	13. Bering Sea
	6. Gulf of Mexico	14. Red Sea
	7. Persian Gulf	15. Bay of
	8. Mediterranean Sea	Bengal
	9. Black Sea	16. Caspian
	10. Baltic Sea	Sea

Area

The area of Earth is about 510 million square kilometers (197 million square miles). Of this, approximately 360 million square kilometers (140 million square miles) are covered by oceans and marginal seas.

2. What percentage of Earth's surface is covered by oceans and marginal seas?

$$\frac{\text{Area of oceans and marginal seas}}{\text{Area of Earth}} \times 100$$

$$= \text{_____} \% \text{ oceans}$$

3. What percentage of Earth's surface is land?
_____ % land

Distribution of Land and Water by Hemisphere

Answer questions 4–7 by examining either a globe, wall map of the world, world map in an atlas, or Figure 2.

4. a. Which hemisphere, Northern or Southern, could be called the "water" hemisphere and which the "land" hemisphere?

"Water" hemisphere: _____

"Land" hemisphere: _____

b. The oceans become (wider, more narrow) as you go from the equator to the pole in the Northern Hemisphere. Circle your answer.

c. In the Southern Hemisphere the width of the oceans (increases, decreases) from the equator to the pole.

5. Follow a line around a globe, world map, and Figure 3 at the latitudes listed on the following page and estimate what percentage of Earth's surface is ocean at each latitude.

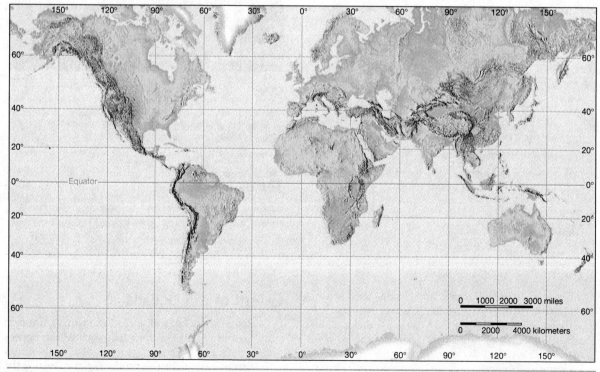

Figure 2 World map.

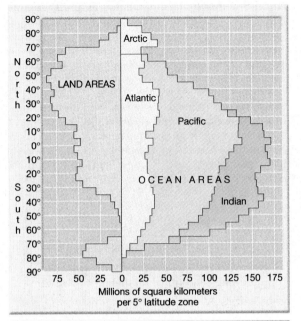

Figure 3 Distribution of land and water in each 5° latitude belt. (After M. Grant Gross, *Oceanography: A View of the Earth*, 2nd ed., Englewood Cliffs, NJ: Prentice-Hall, 1977)

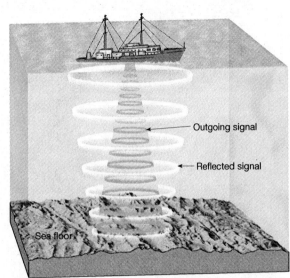

Figure 4 An echo sounder determines the water depth by measuring the time interval required for an acoustic wave to travel from a ship to the seafloor and back. The speed of sound in water is 1,500 m/sec. Therefore, depth = 1/2(1500 m/sec × echo travel time).

	NORTHERN HEMISPHERE	SOUTHERN HEMISPHERE
40°:	_____ % ocean	_____ % ocean
60°:	_____ % ocean	_____ % ocean

6. Which ocean covers the greatest area?

_____

7. Which ocean is almost entirely in the Southern Hemisphere?

_____

Measuring Ocean Depths

Charting the shape or topography of the ocean floor is a fundamental task of oceanographers. In the 1920s a technological breakthrough for determining ocean depths occurred with the invention of electronic depth-sounding equipment. The **echo sounder** (also referred to as *sonar,* an acronym for *so*und *na*vigation *a*nd *r*anging) works by measuring the precise time that a sound wave, traveling at about 1,500 meters per second in water, takes to reach the ocean floor and return to the instrument (Figure 4). Today, in addition to using sophisticated echo sounders such as *multibeam sonar,*

oceanographers are also using satellites to map the ocean floor.

8. Using the formula in Figure 4, calculate the depth of the ocean for each of the following echo soundings.

   5.2 seconds: _____

   6.0 seconds: _____

   2.8 seconds: _____

Ships generally don't make single depth soundings. Rather, as the ship makes a traverse from one location to another, it is continually sending out sound impulses and recording the echoes. In this way, oceanographers obtain many depth recordings from which a *profile* (side view) of the ocean floor can be drawn.

The data in Table 1 were gathered by a ship equipped with an echo sounder as it traveled the North Atlantic Ocean eastward from Cape Cod, Massachusetts. The depths were calculated using the same technique used in question 8.

9. Use the data in Table 1 to construct a generalized profile of the ocean floor in the North Atlantic on Figure 5. Begin by plotting each point at its proper distance from Cape Cod, at the indicated depth. Complete the profile by connecting the depth points.

Table 1   Echo Sounder Depths Eastward
from Cape Cod, MA

POINT	DISTANCE (KM)	DEPTH (M)
1	0	0
2	180	200
3	270	2700
4	420	3300
5	600	4000
6	830	4800
7	1100	4750
8	1130	2500
9	1160	4800
10	1490	4750
11	1770	4800
12	1800	500
13	1830	4850
14	2120	4800
15	2320	4000
16	2650	3000
17	2900	1500
18	2950	1000
19	2960	2700
20	3000	2700
21	3050	1000
22	3130	1900

Ocean Basin Topography

Various features are located along the continental margins and on the ocean basin floor (Figure 6). **Continental shelves**, flooded extensions of the continents, are gently sloping submerged surfaces extending from the shoreline toward the ocean basin. The seaward edge of the continental shelf is marked by the **continental slope**, a relatively steep structure (as compared with the shelf) that marks the boundary between continental crust and oceanic crust. Deep, steep-sided valleys known as **submarine canyons**, eroded in part by the periodic downslope movements of dense, sediment-laden water called **turbidity currents**, are often cut into the continental slope. The ocean basin floor, which constitutes almost 30% of Earth's surface, in-

cludes remarkably flat areas known as **abyssal plains**, tall volcanic peaks called **seamounts**, oceanic plateaus generated by mantle plumes, and **deep-ocean trenches**, which are deep linear depressions that occasionally border some continents, primarily in the Pacific Ocean basin. Near the center of most oceanic basins is a topographically elevated feature, characterized by extensive faulting and numerous volcanic structures, called the **oceanic (or mid-ocean) ridge**. Using Figure 6 and a wall map or atlas as references, briefly describe each of these features in questions 10–15. Label one or more examples of each feature on Figure 5 and the ocean floor map of the North Atlantic Ocean basin, Figure 7.

10. Continental shelf: _____

_____

   a. What is the approximate average ocean depth along the continental shelves bordering North America?

   _____

   b. Write a brief statement comparing the width of the continental shelf along the east coast, west coast, and gulf coast of North America.

   _____

   _____

11. Continental slope: _____

_____

   a. Briefly describe the origin of submarine canyons and label at least one on Figure 7.

   _____

   _____

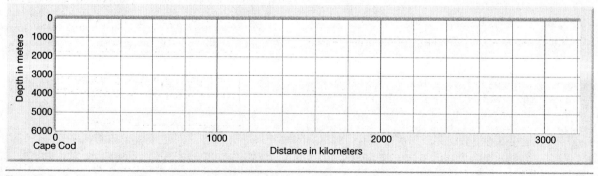

Figure 5   North Atlantic Ocean floor profile (exaggerated).

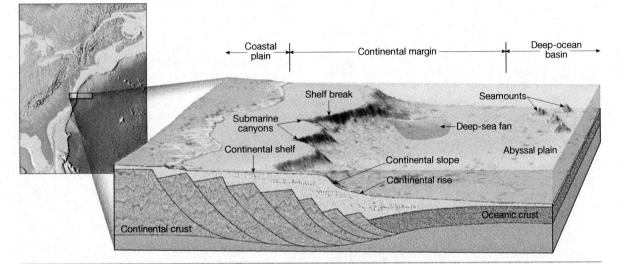

Figure 6 Generalized continental margin. Note that the slopes shown for the continental shelf and continental slope are greatly exaggerated. The continental shelf has an average slope of one tenth of 1 degree, while the continental slope has an average of about 5 degrees.

12. Abyssal plain: _____

_____

 a. The general topography of abyssal plains is (flat, irregular). Circle your answer.

 b. How do abyssal plains form and what is their composition?

 _____

 _____

13. Seamount: _____

14. Deep-ocean trench (not shown on Figure 5):

 _____

 _____

 _____

 a. Approximately how deep is the Puerto Rico trench?

 _____ meters

 b. Use a map or globe to locate three deep-ocean trenches in the western Pacific Ocean. Give the name, location, and depth of each.

Trench 1: _____

_____

Trench 2: _____

_____

Trench 3: _____

_____

15. Mid-ocean ridge: _____

_____

 a. Examine the mid-ocean ridge system on a world map. Follow the ridge eastward from the Atlantic Ocean into the Indian Ocean and then into the Pacific. Describe what happens to the ridge along the southwest coast of North America.

 _____

 b. Approximately how high above the adjacent ocean floor does the Mid-Atlantic Ridge rise?

 _____ meters

16. Note that Figures 5 and 7 illustrate only the western side of the North Atlantic floor. Using a globe or map, write a brief statement comparing the to-

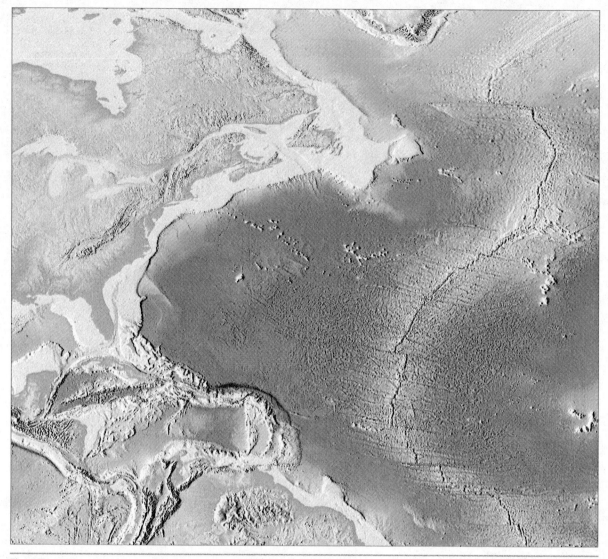

Figure 7 North Atlantic basin.

pography of the North Atlantic Ocean floor east of the mid-ocean ridge to that on the west side.

_____

_____

_____

_____

Characteristics of Ocean Water

Ocean circulation has two primary components: surface ocean currents and deep-ocean circulation. While

surface currents like the famous Gulf Stream are driven primarily by the prevailing world winds, the deep-ocean circulation is largely the result of differences in ocean water **density** (mass per unit volume of a substance). A **density current** is the movement (flow) of one body of water over, under, or through another caused by density differences and gravity. Variations in **salinity** and temperature are the two most important factors in creating the density differences that result in the deep-ocean circulation.

Salinity

Salinity is the amount of dissolved solid material in water, expressed as parts per thousand parts of water. The symbol for parts per thousand is 0/00. Although

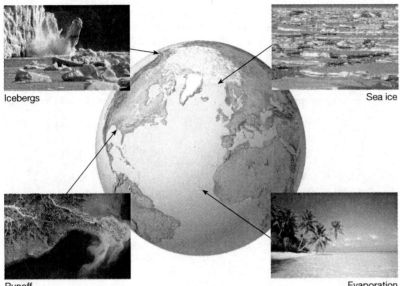

Icebergs

Sea ice

Runoff

Evaporation

Figure 8 Processes affecting seawater salinity. Processes that *decrease* seawater salinity include precipitation, runoff, icebergs melting, and sea ice melting. Processes that *increase* seawater salinity include formation of sea ice and evaporation. Source: (upper left) Tom Bean/Tom and Susan Bean, Inc., (upper right) Wolfgang Kaehler Photography, (lower left) NASA Headquarters, (lower right) Paul Steel/Corbis/Stock Market.

there are many dissolved salts in seawater, sodium chloride (common table salt) is the most abundant.

Variations in the salinity of seawater are primarily a consequence of changes in the water content of the solution. In regions where evaporation is high, the proportionate amount of dissolved material in seawater is increased by removing the water and leaving behind the salts. On the other hand, in areas of high precipitation and high runoff, the additional water dilutes seawater and lowers the salinity. Since the factors that determine the concentration of salts in seawater are not constant from the equator to the poles, the salinity of seawater also varies with latitude and depth (Figure 8).

Salinity–Density Experiment

To gain a better understanding of how salinity affects the density of water, examine the equipment in the lab (see Figure 9) and conduct the following experiment by completing each of the indicated steps.

Step 1. Fill the measuring cylinder with cool tap water up to the rubber band or other marker near the top of the cylinder.

Step 2. Fill a test tube about half full of solution A (saltwater) and pour it slowly into the cylinder. Observe and describe what happens.

Observations: _____

_____

Step 3. Repeat steps 1 and 2 two additional times and measure the time required for the front edge of the saltwater to travel from the rubber band to the bottom of the cylinder. Record the times

for each test in the data table, Table 2. *Make certain* that you drain the cylinder after each trial and refill it with fresh water and use the same amount of solution with each trial.

Step 4. Determine the travel time two times for solution B exactly as you did with solution A and enter your measurements in Table 2.

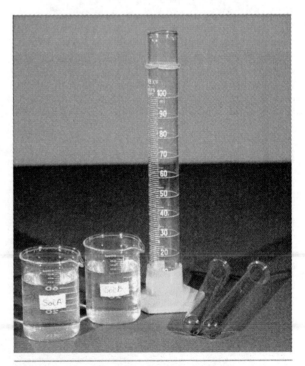

Figure 9 Lab setup for salinity–density experiment.

Table 2   Salinity–Density Experiment Data Table

SOLUTION	TIMED TRIAL #1	TIMED TRIAL #2	AVERAGE OF BOTH TRIALS
A			
B			
Solution B plus salt		XXXX	XXXX

Step 5. Fill a test tube about half full of solution B and add to it some additional salt. Then shake the test tube vigorously. Determine the travel time of this solution and enter your results in Table 2.

Step 6. Clean all your glassware.

17. Questions 17a and 17b refer to the salinity–density experiment.

   a. Write a brief summary of the results of your salinity–density experiment.

   _____

   _____

   b. Since the solution that traveled fastest has the greatest density, solution (A, B) is most dense. Circle your answer.

     Table 3 lists the approximate surface water salinity at various latitudes in the Atlantic and Pacific Oceans. Using the data, construct a salinity curve for each ocean on the graph, Figure 10. *Use a different-colored pencil for each ocean.* Then answer questions 18–22.

Table 3   Ocean Surface Water Salinity in Parts per Thousand (0/00) at Various Latitudes in the Atlantic and Pacific Oceans

LATITUDE	ATLANTIC OCEAN	PACIFIC OCEAN
60°N	33.0 0/00	31.0 0/00
50°	33.7	32.5
40°	34.8	33.2
30°	36.7	34.2
20°	36.8	34.2
10°	36.0	34.4
0°	35.0	34.3
10°	35.9	35.2
20°	36.7	35.6
30°	36.2	35.7
40°	35.3	35.0
50°	34.3	34.4
60°S	33.9	34.0

18. At which latitudes are the highest surface salinities located?

   _____

19. What are two factors that control the concentration of salts in seawater?

   _____ and _____

20. Refer to the factors listed in question 19. What is the cause of the difference in surface water salinity between equatorial and subtropical regions in the Atlantic Ocean?

   _____

   _____

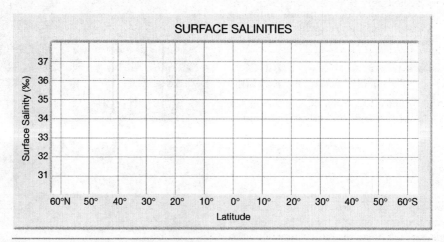

Figure 10 Graph for plotting surface salinities.

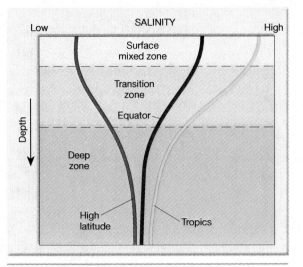

Figure 11 Ocean water salinity changes with depth at high latitudes, equatorial regions, and the tropics.

21. Of the two oceans, the (Atlantic, Pacific) Ocean has higher average surface salinities. Circle your answer.

22. Suggest a reason(s) for the difference in average surface salinities between the oceans.

_____

_____

_____

Figure 11 shows how ocean water salinity varies with depth at different latitudes. Use the figure to answer questions 23–26.

23. In general, salinity (increases, decreases) with depth in the equatorial and tropical regions and (increases, decreases) with depth at high latitudes. Circle your answers.

24. Why are the surface salinities higher than the deepwater salinities in the lower latitudes?

_____

The *halocline* (*halo*-salt, *cline*-slope) is a layer of ocean water where there is a rapid change in salinity with depth.

25. Label the halocline on Figure 11. Where does it occur?

_____

26. Below the halocline the salinity of ocean water (increases rapidly, remains fairly constant, decreases rapidly). Circle your answer.

Ocean Water Temperatures

Seawater temperature is the most extensively determined variable of the oceans because it is easily measured and has an important influence on marine life. Like salinity, ocean water temperatures vary from the equator to poles and also changes with depth.

Temperature, like salinity, also affects the density of seawater. However, the density of seawater is more sensitive to temperature fluctuations than salinity.

Temperature–Density Experiment

To illustrate the effects of temperature on the density of water, examine the equipment in the lab (see Figure 12) and then conduct the following experiment by completing each of the indicated steps.

Step 1. Fill a measuring cylinder with *cold* tap water up to the rubber band.

Step 2. Put 2–3 drops of dye in a test tube and fill it half full with *hot* tap water.

Step 3. Pour the contents of the test tube *slowly* into the cylinder and then record your observations.

Observations: _____

_____

_____

Figure 12 Lab setup for temperature–density experiment.

Step 4. Empty the cylinder and refill it with *hot* water.

Step 5. Add a test tube full of cold water and 2–3 drops of dye to some ice in a beaker. Stir the solution for a few seconds. Fill the test tube three-fourths full with some liquid (no ice) from your beaker. Pour this cold liquid *slowly* into the cylinder. Then record your observations.

Observations: _____

_____

_____

Step 6. Clean the glassware and return it along with the other materials to your instructor.

27. Questions 27a and 27b refer to the temperature–density experiment.

    a. Write a brief summary of your temperature–density experiment.

_____

_____

_____

    b. Given equal salinities, (cold, warm) seawater would have the greatest density. Circle your answer.

Table 4 shows the average surface temperature and density of seawater at various latitudes. Using the data, plot a line on the graph in Figure 13 for temperature and a separate line for density using a different color. Then answer questions 28–30.

28. (Warm, Cool) surface temperatures and (high, low) surface densities occur in the equatorial regions. While at high latitudes, (warm, cool) surface temperatures and (high, low) surface densities are found. Circle your answers.

Table 4   Idealized Ocean Surface Water Temperatures and Densities at Various Latitudes

LATITUDE	SURFACE TEMPERATURE (C°)	SURFACE DENSITY (g/cm³)
60°N	5	1.0258
40°	13	1.0259
20°	24	1.0237
0°	27	1.0238
20°	24	1.0241
40°	15	1.0261
60°S	2	1.0272

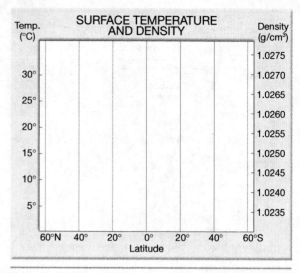

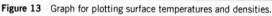

Figure 13   Graph for plotting surface temperatures and densities.

29. What is the reason for the fact that higher average surface densities are found in the Southern Hemisphere?

_____

In question 18 you concluded that surface salinities were greatest at about latitudes 30°N and 30°S.

30. Refer to the density curve in Figure 13. What evidence supports the fact that the temperature of seawater is more of a controlling factor of density than salinity?

_____

_____

Figure 14 shows how ocean water temperature varies with depth at different latitudes. Use the figure to answer questions 31–33.

31. Temperature decreases most rapidly with depth at (high, low) latitudes. Circle your answer and give the reason that the decrease with depth is most rapid at these latitudes.

_____

The layer of water where there is a rapid change of temperature with depth is called the *thermocline* (*thermo* = heat, *cline* = slope). The thermocline is a very important structure in the ocean because it creates a vertical barrier to many types of marine life.

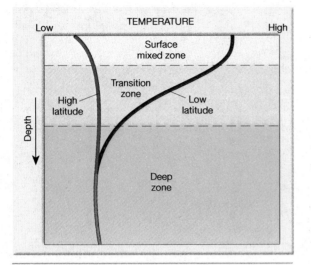

Figure 14 Ocean water temperature changes with depth at high and low latitudes.

32. Label the thermocline on Figure 14. Where does it occur?

_____

33. Below the thermocline the temperature of ocean water (increases rapidly, remains fairly constant, decreases rapidly). Circle your answer.

Oceanography on the Internet

Continue your exploration of the oceans by applying the concepts in this exercise to investigate real-time ocean water characteristics on the *Applications & Investigations in Earth Science* website at http://prenhall.com/earthsciencelab

Notes and calculations.

Introduction to Oceanography

Date Due: _____

Name: _____

Date: _____

Class: _____

After you have finished this exercise, complete the following questions. You may have to refer to the exercise for assistance or to locate specific answers. Be prepared to submit this summary/report to your instructor at the designated time.

1. Give the approximate latitude and longitude of the centers of each of the following water bodies.

   Mediterranean Sea: _____

   Sea of Japan: _____

   Indian Ocean: _____

2. Write a brief statement comparing the distribution of water and land in the Northern Hemisphere to the distribution in the Southern Hemisphere.

   _____

   _____.

3. On the ocean basin profile in Figure 15, label the continental shelf, continental slope, abyssal plain, seamounts, mid-ocean ridge, and deep-ocean trench.

4. List the names and depths of two Pacific Ocean trenches.

NAME	DEPTH
_____	_____
_____	_____

5. Explain how an echo sounder is used to determine the shape or topography of the ocean floor.

   _____

   _____

   _____

   _____

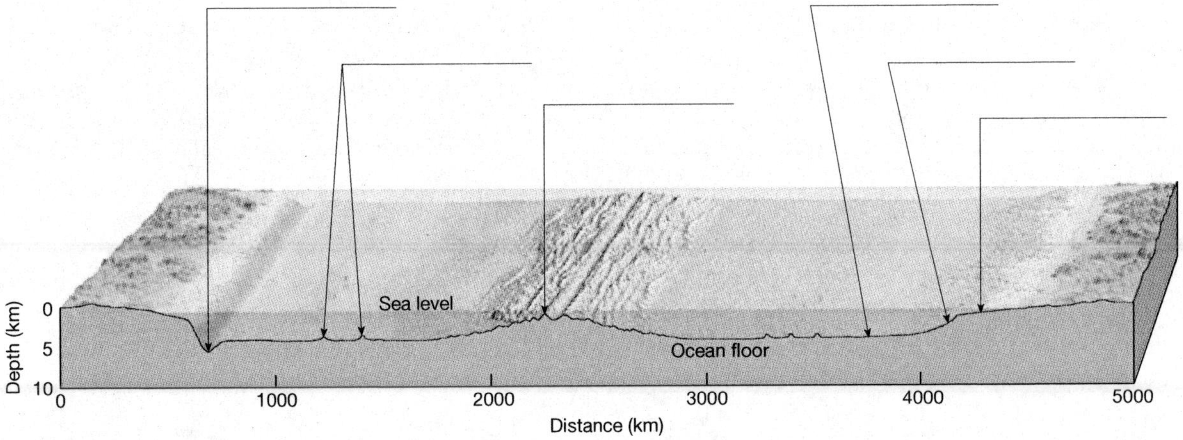

Figure 15 Hypothetical ocean basin.

6. The following are some short statements. Circle the most appropriate response.

   a. The higher the salinity of seawater, the (lower, higher) the density.

   b. The lower the temperature of seawater, the (lower, higher) the density.

   c. Surface salinity is greatest in (polar, subtropical, equatorial) regions.

   d. (Temperature, Salinity) has the greatest influence on the density of seawater.

   e. (Warm, Cold) seawater with (high, low) salinity would have the greatest density.

   f. Vertical movements of ocean water are most likely to begin in (equatorial, subtropical, polar) regions, because the surface water there is (most, least) dense.

7. Summarize the results of your salinity–density and temperature–density experiments.

   Salinity–density experiment: _____

   _____

   _____

   _____

   Temperature–density experiment: _____

   _____

   _____

   _____

8. Why is the surface salinity of an ocean higher in the subtropics than in the equatorial regions?

   _____

   _____

   _____

9. Given your understanding of the relation between ocean water temperature, salinity, and density, where in the Atlantic Ocean would you expect surface water to sink and initiate a subsurface flow? List the reason(s) for your choice(s).

   _____

   _____

   _____

   _____

10. Refer to the salinity–density experiment you conducted. Solution (A, B) had the greatest density. Circle your answer.

11. Describe the change in salinity *and* temperature with depth that occurs at low latitudes.

    Salinity: _____

    _____

    _____

    Temperature: _____

    _____

    _____

12. Are the following statements true or false? Circle your response. If the statement is false, correct the word(s) so that it reads as a true statement.

    T F a. The Atlantic Ocean covers the greatest area of all the world oceans.

    T F b. Continental shelves are part of the deep-ocean floor.

    T F c. Deep-ocean trenches are located in the middle of ocean basins.

    T F d. High evaporation rates in the subtropics cause the surface ocean water to have a lower than average salinity.

12

Determining Geologic Ages

The recognition of the vastness of geologic time and the ability to establish the sequence of geologic events that have occurred at various places at different times are among the great intellectual achievements of science. To accomplish the task of deciphering Earth's history, geologists have formulated several laws, principles, and doctrines that can be used to place geologic events in their proper sequence (Figure 1). Also, using the principles that govern the radioactive decay of certain elements, scientists are now able to determine the age of many Earth materials with reasonable accuracy. In this exercise you will investigate some of the techniques and procedures used by Earth scientists in their search to interpret the geologic history of Earth.

Objectives

After you have completed this exercise, you should be able to:

1. List and explain each of the laws, principles, and doctrines that are used to determine the relative ages of geologic events.

2. Determine the sequence of geologic events that have occurred in an area by applying the techniques and procedures for relative dating.

3. Explain the methods of fossilization and how fossils are used to define the ages of rocks and correlate rock units.

4. Explain how the radioactive decay of certain elements can be used to determine the age of Earth materials.

5. Apply the techniques of radiometric dating to determine the numerical age of a rock.

6. Describe the geologic time scale and list in proper order some of the major events that have taken place on Earth since its formation.

Figure 1 In any sequence of underformed sedimentary rocks, the oldest rock is always at the bottom and the youngest is at the top. (Photo by E. J. Tarbuck)

Materials

ruler   calculator

Materials Supplied by Your Instructor

fossils and fossil questions   meterstick or metric
 (optional)   tape measure
5-meter length of adding-
 machine paper

Terms

relative dating   unconformity   radiometric
uniformitarianism cross-cutting   date
original   fossil   half-life
 horizontality   fossil succession   eon
superposition   era
inclusion

Relative Dating

Relative dating, the placing of geologic events in their proper sequence or order, does not tell how long ago something occurred, only that it preceded one event and followed another. Several logical doctrines, laws, and principles govern the techniques used to establish the relative age of an object or event.

Doctrine of Uniformitarianism

First proposed by James Hutton in the late 1700s, this doctrine states that the physical, chemical, and biological laws that operate today have operated throughout Earth's history. Although geologic processes such as erosion, deposition, and volcanism are governed by these unchanging laws, their rates and intensities may vary. The doctrine is often summarized in the statement, "The present is the key to the past."

Principle of Original Horizontality

Sediment, when deposited, forms nearly horizontal layers. Therefore, if we observe beds of sedimentary rocks that are folded or inclined at a steep angle, the implication is that some deforming force took place after the sediment was deposited (Figure 2).

Law of Superposition

In any sequence of undeformed sedimentary rocks (or surface deposited igneous rocks such as lava flows and layers of volcanic ash), the oldest rock is always at the bottom and the youngest is at the top. Therefore, each layer of rock represents an interval of time that is more recent than that of the underlying rocks (see Figure 1).

Figure 2   Uplifted and tilted sedimentary strata in the Canadian Rockies. (Photo by E. J. Tarbuck)

Figure 3   Sequence of playing cards illustrating the law of superposition.

Assume the playing cards shown in Figure 3 are layers of sedimentary rocks viewed from above.

1. In the space provided in Figure 3, list the order, first (oldest) to last (youngest), in which the cards were laid down.

2. Were you able to place all of the cards in sequence? If not, which one(s) could not be "relative" dated and why?

_____

_____

Figure 4 illustrates a geologic cross section, a side view, of the rocks beneath the surface of a hypothetical region. Use Figure 4 to answer questions 3 and 4.

3. Of the two sequences of rocks, A–D and E–G (A–D, E–G), was disturbed by crustal movements after its deposition. Circle your answer. What law or principle did you apply to arrive at your answer?

_____

4. Apply the law of superposition to determine the relative ages of the *undisturbed* sequence of sedimentary rocks. List the letter of the oldest rock layer first.

Oldest _____ Youngest

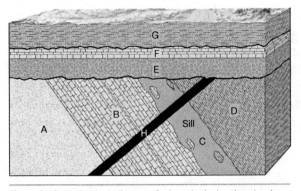

Figure 4 Geologic block diagram of a hypothetical region showing igneous intrusive features (C and H) and sedimentary rocks.

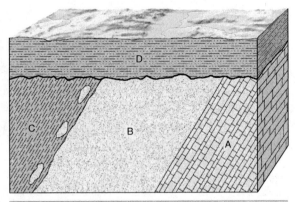

Figure 6 Geologic block diagram showing sedimentary rocks.

Inclusions

Inclusions are pieces of one rock unit that are contained within another unit (Figure 5). The rock mass adjacent to the one containing the inclusions must have been there first in order to provide the rock fragments. Therefore, the rock containing the inclusions is the younger of the two.

Refer to Figure 6 to answer questions 5 and 6. The sedimentary layer B is a sandstone. Letter C is the sedimentary rock, shale.

5. Identify and label the inclusions in Figure 6.
6. Of the two rocks B and C, rock (B, C) is older. Circle your answer.

Unconformities

As long as continuous sedimentation occurs at a particular place, there will be an uninterrupted record of the material and life forms. However, if the sedimentation process is suspended by an emergence of the area from below sea level, then no sediment will be deposited and

Figure 5 Inclusions are fragments of one rock enclosed within another. (Photo by E. J. Tarbuck)

an erosion surface will develop. The result is that no rock record will exist for a part of geologic time. Such a gap in the rock record is termed an **unconformity**. An unconformity is typically shown on a cross-sectional (side view) diagram by a wavy line ($\sim\sim$). Several types of unconformities are illustrated in Figure 7.

7. Identify and label an example of an angular unconformity and a disconformity in Figure 4.

Principle of Cross-Cutting Relationships

Whenever a fault or intrusive igneous rock cuts through an existing feature, it is younger than the structure it cuts. For example, if a basalt dike cuts through a sandstone layer, the sandstone had to be there first and, therefore, is older than the dike (Figure 8).

Figure 9 is a geologic cross section showing sedimentary rocks (A, B, D, E, F, and G), an igneous intrusive feature called a *dike* (C), and a *fault* (H). Use Figure 9 to answer questions 8–11.

8. The igneous intrusion C is (older, younger) than the sedimentary rocks B and D. Circle your answer.
9. Fault H is (older, younger) than the sedimentary beds A–E.
10. The relative age of fault H is (older, younger) than the sedimentary layer F.
11. Did the fault occur before or after the igneous intrusion? Explain how you arrived at your answer.

_____

_____

12. Refer to Figure 4. The igneous intrusion H is (older, younger) than rock layer E and (older, younger) than layer D. Circle your answers.
13. Refer to Figure 4. What evidence supports the conclusion that the igneous intrusive feature

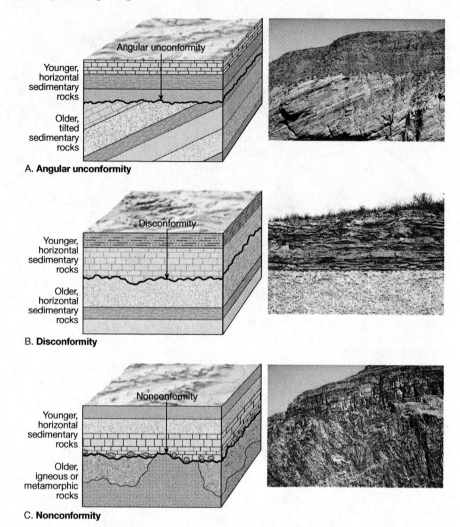

A. **Angular unconformity**

Angular unconformity

Younger, horizontal sedimentary rocks

Older, tilted sedimentary rocks

Disconformity

Younger, horizontal sedimentary rocks

Older, horizontal sedimentary rocks

B. **Disconformity**

Nonconformity

Younger, horizontal sedimentary rocks

Older, igneous or metamorphic rocks

C. **Nonconformity**

Figure 7   Three common types of unconformities. On the diagrams, wavy dashed lines mark the unconformity.

Figure 8   This basalt dike (black) is younger than the sandstone layers that it cuts through. (Photo by E. J. Tarbuck)

called a *sill*, C, is more recent than both of the rock layers B and D and older than the igneous intrusion H?

Fossils and the Principle of Fossil Succession

Fossils (Figure 10) are among the most important tools used to interpret Earth's history. They are used to define the ages of rocks, correlate one rock unit with another, and determine past environments on Earth.

Earth has been inhabited by different assemblages of plants and animals at different times. As rocks form, they often incorporate the preserved remains of these organisms as fossils. According to the principle of **fossil succession**, fossil organisms succeed each other in a definite and determinable order. Therefore, the time that a rock originated can frequently be determined by noting the kinds of fossils that are found within it.

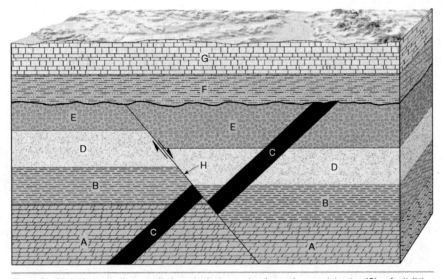

Figure 9   Geologic block diagram of a hypothetical area showing an igneous intrusion (C), a fault (H), and sedimentary rocks.

Figure 10   Various types of fossilization. In photo **A.** the mineral quartz now occupies the internal spaces of what was once wood. **B.** is the replica of fish after the carbonized remains were removed. In photo **C.** mineral matter occupies the hollow space where a shell was once located. **D.** is a track left by a dinosaur in formerly soft sediment. (Photos by E. J. Tarbuck)

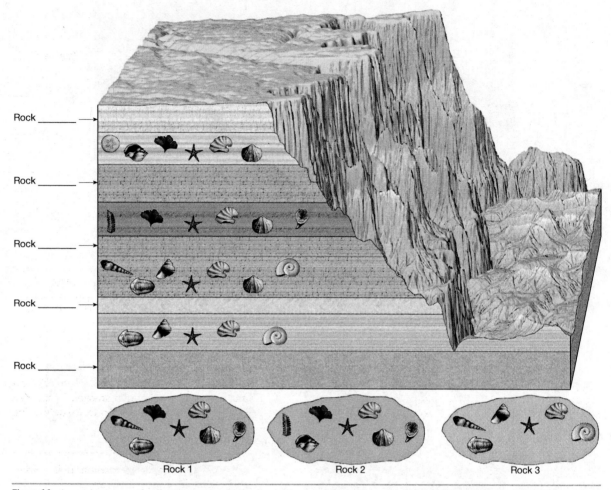

Rock _____

Rock _____

Rock _____

Rock _____

Rock _____

Rock 1   Rock 2   Rock 3

Figure 11 Layered sequence of sedimentary rocks with fossils and three separate rocks containing similar fossils.

Using the materials supplied by your instructor, answer questions 14 and 15.

14. At the discretion of your instructor, there may be several stations with fossils and questions set up in the laboratory. Following the specific directions of your instructor, proceed to the stations.

15. What are the conditions that would favor the preservation of an organism as a fossil?

_____

_____

16. Refer to Figure 10. Select the photo, A, B, C, or D, that best illustrates each of the following methods of fossilization or fossil evidence.

Petrification: The small internal cavities and pores of the original organism are filled with precipitated mineral matter. Photo: _____

Cast: The space once occupied by a dissolved shell or other structure is subsequently filled with mineral matter. Photo: _____

Impression: A replica of a former fossil left in fine-grained sediment after the fossilizing material, often carbon, is removed. Photo: _____

Indirect evidence: Traces of prehistoric life, but not the organism itself. Photo: _____

Figure 11 shows a sequence of undeformed sedimentary rocks. Each layer of rock contains the fossils illustrated within it. The three rocks, Rocks 1, 2, and 3, illustrated below the layered sequence were found nearby and each rock contains the fossils indicated. Answer question 17 using Figure 11.

17. Applying the principle of fossil succession, indicate the proper position of each of the three rocks relative to the rock layers by writing the words Rock 1, Rock 2, or Rock 3 at the appropriate position in the sequence.

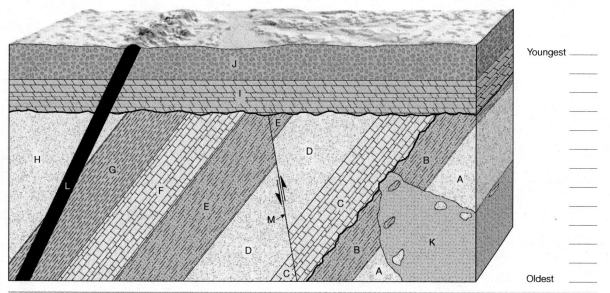

Figure 12 Geologic block diagram of a hypothetical area showing igneous intrusive features (K and L), a fault (M), and sedimentary rocks.

Applying Relative Dating Techniques

Geologists often apply several of the techniques of relative dating when investigating the geologic history of an area.

Figure 12 is a geologic cross section of a hypothetical area. Letters K and L are igneous rocks. Letter M is a fault. All the remaining letters represent sedimentary rocks. Using Figure 12 to complete questions 18–24 will provide insight into how the relative geologic history of an area is determined.

18. Identify and label the unconformities indicated in the cross section.

19. Rock layer I is (older, younger) than layer J. Circle your answer. What law or principle have you applied to determine your answer?

_____

_____

20. The fault is (older, younger) than rock layer I. Circle your answer. What law or principle have you applied to determine your answer?

_____

_____

_____

21. The igneous intrusion K is (older, younger) than layers A and B. Circle your answer. What two laws or principles have you applied to determine your answer?

_____ and _____

22. The age of the igneous intrusion L is (older, younger) than layers J, I, H, G, and F.

23. List the entire sequence of events, in order from oldest to youngest, by writing the appropriate letter in the space provided on the figure.

24. Explain why it was difficult to place the fault, letter M, in a specific position among the sequence of events in Figure 12.

_____

_____

_____

_____

_____

_____

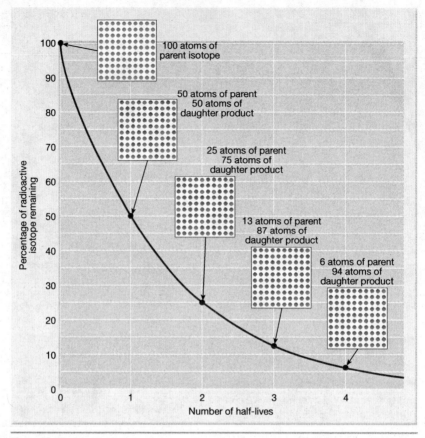

Figure 13 Radioactive decay curve.

Radiometric Dating

The discovery of radioactivity and its subsequent understanding has provided a reliable means for calculating the *numerical age* in years of many Earth materials. Radioactive atoms, such as the isotope uranium-238, emit particles from their nuclei that we detect as radiation. Ultimately, this process of decay produces an atom that is stable and no longer radioactive. For example, eventually the stable atom lead-206 is produced from the radioactive decay of uranium-238.

Determining Radiometric Ages

The radioactive isotope used to determine a **radiometric date** is referred to as the *parent isotope*. The amount of time it takes for half of the radioactive nuclei in a sample to change to their stable end product is referred to as the **half-life** of the isotope. The isotopes resulting from the decay of the parent are termed the *daughter products*. For example, if we begin with one gram of radioactive material, half a gram would decay and become a daughter product after one half-life. After the second half-life, half

of the remaining radioactive isotope, 0.25 g or $\frac{1}{4}$ of the original amount $\left(\frac{1}{2} \text{ of } \frac{1}{2}\right)$, would still exist. *With each successive half-life, the remaining parent isotope would be reduced by half.*

Figure 13 graphically illustrates how the ratio of a parent isotope to its stable daughter product continually changes with time. Use Figure 13 to help answer questions 25–29.

25. What percentage of the original parent isotope remains after each of the following half-lives has elapsed?

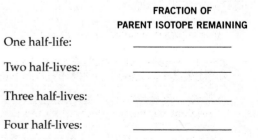

One half-life: _____

Two half-lives: _____

Three half-lives: _____

Four half-lives: _____

26. Assume you begin with 10.0 g of a radioactive parent isotope. How many grams of parent isotope will be present in the sample after each of the following half-lives?

REMAINING PARENT ISOTOPE

One half-life: _____ g

Four half-lives: _____ g

27. If a radioactive isotope has a half-life of 400 million years, how long will it take for 50% of the material to change to the daughter product?

_____ years

28. A sample is brought to the laboratory and the chemist determines that the percentage of the parent isotope remaining is 13% of the total amount that was originally present. If the half-life of the material is 600 million years, how old is the sample?

_____ years old

29. Determine the numerical ages of rock samples that contain a parent isotope with a half-life of 100 million years and have the following percentages of original parent isotope.

50%:   Age = _____

25%:   Age = _____

6%:   Age = _____

Applying Radiometric Dates

When used in conjunction with relative dates, radiometric dates help Earth scientists refine their interpretation of the geologic history of an area. Completing questions 30–35 will aid in understanding how both types of dates are often used together.

Previously in the exercise you determined the geologic history of the area represented in Figure 12 using relative dating techniques. Assume that the rock layers H and I in Figure 12 each contain radioactive materials with known half-lives.

30. An analysis of a sample of rock from layer H indicates an equal proportion of parent isotope and daughter produced from the parent. The half-life of the parent is known to be 425 million years.

   a. (Fifty, Twenty-five, Thirteen) percent of the original parent has decayed to the daughter product. Circle your answer.

   b. How many half-lives of the parent isotope have elapsed since rock H formed?

   _____

   c. What is the numerical age of rock layer H? Write your answer below and at rock layer H on Figure 12.

   Age of rock layer H = _____ years

31. The analysis of a sample of rock from layer I indicates its age to be 400 million years. Write the numerical age of layer I on Figure 12.

Refer to the relative and numerical ages you determined for the rocks in Figure 12 to answer the following questions.

32. How many years long is the interval of time represented by the unconformity that separates rock layer H from layer I? Explain how you arrived at your answer.

   The unconformity represents an interval of time that was _____ million years long.

   Explanation: _____

   _____

   _____

   _____

33. The age of fault M is (older, younger) than 400 million years. Circle your answer. Explain how you arrived at your answer.

   Explanation: _____

   _____

   _____

   _____

34. What is the approximate maximum numerical age of the igneous intrusion L?

   The igneous intrusion L formed more recently than _____ million years ago.

35. Complete the following general statement describing the numerical ages of rock layers G, F, and E.

   All of the rock layers are (younger, older) than _____ million years.

The Geologic Time Scale

Applying the techniques of geologic dating, the history of Earth has been subdivided into several different units which provide a meaningful time frame within which the events of the geologic past are arranged. Since the span of a human life is but a "blink of an eye" compared to the age of Earth, it is often difficult to comprehend the magnitude of geologic time. By completing questions 36–41, you will be better able to grasp the great age of Earth and appreciate the sequence of events that have brought it to this point in time.

36. Obtain a piece of adding machine paper slightly longer than 5 meters and a meterstick or metric measuring tape from your instructor. Draw a line at one end of the paper and label it "PRESENT." Using the following scale, construct a time line by completing the indicated steps.

SCALE

1 meter = 1 billion years

10 centimeters = 100 million years

1 centimeter = 10 million years

1 millimeter = 1 million years

Step 1. Using the geologic time scale, Figure 14, as a reference, divide your time line into the **eons** and **eras** of geologic time. Label each division with its name and indicate its absolute age.

Step 2. Using the scale, plot and label the plant and animal events listed in Figure 14 on your time line.

After completing your time line, answer questions 37–41.

37. What fraction or percent of geologic time is represented by the Precambrian eon?

Approximately _____ of geologic time.

38. Suggest a reason(s) why approximately 542 million years ago was selected to mark the end of Proterozoic eon and the beginning of the Paleozoic era.

_____

_____

_____

_____

_____

39. Write a brief statement outlining the various life forms that have existed on Earth through time.

_____

_____

_____

40. How many times longer is the whole of geologic time than the time represented by recorded history, about 5,000 years?

Geologic time is _____ times longer than recorded history.

41. For what fraction or percent of geologic time have land plants been present on Earth?

Approximately _____ of geologic time.

Geologic Time on the Internet

Apply what you have learned in this exercise to write a geologic interpretation of a rock outcrop and to explore the fossil record by completing the corresponding on-line activities on the *Applications & Investigations in Earth Science* website at http://prenhall.com/earthsciencelab

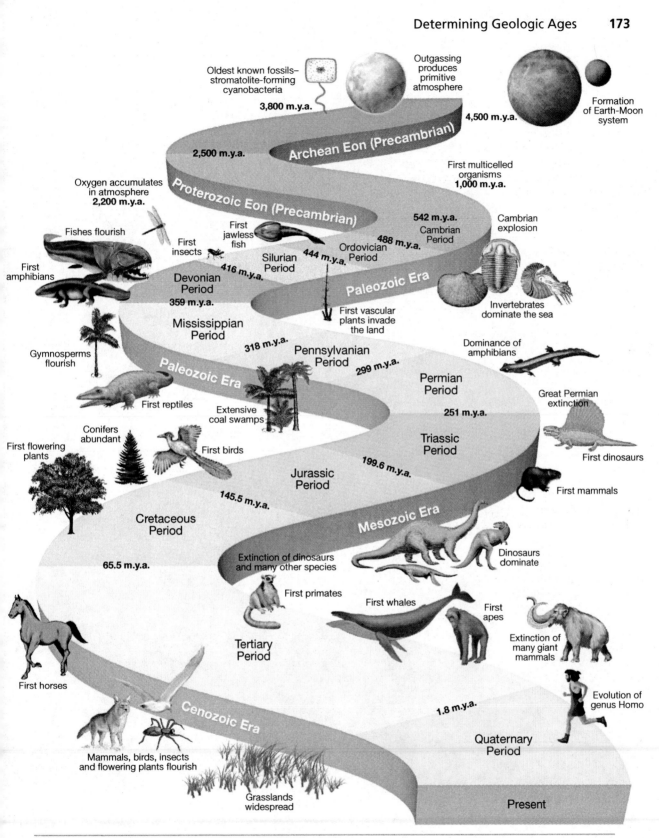

Figure 14   The geologic time scale. (Data from the Geologic Society of America)

Notes and calculations.

Determining Geologic Ages

Date Due: _____

Name: _____

Date: _____

Class: _____

After you have finished this exercise, complete the following questions. You may have to refer to the exercise for assistance or to locate specific answers. Be prepared to submit this summary/report to your instructor at the designated time.

1. Determine the sequence of geologic events that have occurred at the hypothetical area illustrated in Figure 15. List your answers from oldest to youngest in the space provided by the figure. Letters M and N are faults, J, K, and L are igneous intrusions, and all other layers are sedimentary rocks.

2. The following questions refer to Figure 15.

   a. What type of unconformity separates layer G from layer F?

   _____

   b. Which law, principle, or doctrine of relative dating did you apply to determine that rock layer H is older than layer I?

   _____

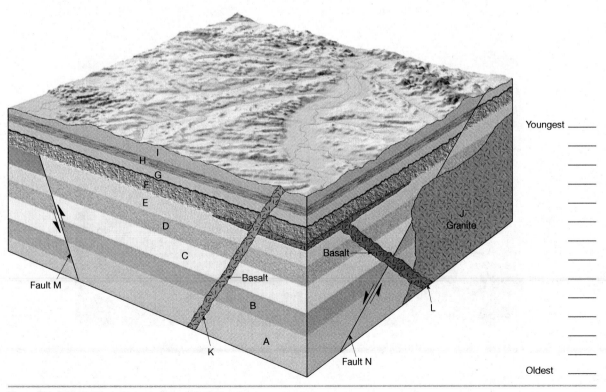

Figure 15 Geologic block diagram of a hypothetical region.

c. Which law, principle, or doctrine of relative dating did you apply to determine that fault M is older than rock layer F?

_____

d. Explain why you know that fault N is older than the igneous intrusion J.

_____

e. If rock layer F is 150 million years old and layer E is 160 million years old, what is the approximate age of fault M?

_____ million years

f. The analysis of samples from layers G and F indicates the following proportions of parent isotope to the daughter product produced from it. If the half-life of the parent is known to be 75 million years, what are the ages of the two layers?

	PARENT	DAUGHTER	AGE
Layer G:	50%	50%	_____
Layer F:	25%	75%	_____

g. What absolute time interval is represented by the unconformity at the base of rock layer G?

From _____ to _____ million years

3. List the sequence of geologic events that you determined took place in the area represented by Figure 12, question 23, in the exercise.

Oldest _____ Youngest

4. What fraction of time is represented by each of the following geologic eons?

Phanerozoic eon: _____ Precambrian eon: _____

5. How many meters long would the time line you constructed in the exercise, question 36, have been if you had used a scale of 1 millimeter equals 1,000 years?

_____

6. Examine the photograph in Figure 16 closely. Applying the principles of relative dating, describe as accurately as possible the relative geologic history of the area.

_____

_____

_____

_____

Figure 16 Photo of sedimentary beds to be used with question 6. (Photo by E. J. Tarbuck)

Metric and English Units Compared

Units

1 kilometer (km)	=	1000 meters (m)
1 meter (m)	=	100 centimeters (cm)
1 centimeter (cm)	=	0.39 inch (in.)
1 mile (mi)	=	5280 feet (ft)
1 foot (ft)	=	12 inches (in.)
1 inch (in.)	=	2.54 centimeters (cm)
1 square mile (mi^2)	=	640 acres (a)
1 kilogram (kg)	=	1000 grams (g)
1 pound (lb)	=	16 ounces (oz)
1 fathom	=	6 feet (ft)

Conversions

When you want
to convert: multiply by: to find:

Length

inches	2.54	centimeters
centimeters	0.39	inches
feet	0.30	meters
meters	3.28	feet
yards	0.91	meters
meters	1.09	yards
miles	1.61	kilometers
kilometers	0.62	miles

Area

square inches	6.45	square centimeters
square centimeters	0.15	square inches
square feet	0.09	square meters
square meters	10.76	square feet
square miles	2.59	square kilometers
square kilometers	0.39	square miles

When you want
to convert: multiply by: to find:

Volume

cubic inches	16.38	cubic centimeters
cubic centimeters	0.06	cubic inches
cubic feet	0.028	cubic meters
cubic meters	35.3	cubic feet
cubic miles	4.17	cubic kilometers
cubic kilometers	0.24	cubic miles
liters	1.06	quarts
liters	0.26	gallons
gallons	3.78	liters

Masses and Weights

ounces	20.33	grams
grams	0.035	ounces
pounds	0.45	kilograms
kilograms	2.205	pounds

Temperature

When you want to convert degrees Fahrenheit (°F) to degrees Celsius (°C), subtract 32 degrees and divide by 1.8

When you want to convert degrees Celsius (°C) to degrees Fahrenheit (°F), multiply by 1.8 and add 32 degrees.

When you want to convert degrees Celsius (°C) to kelvins (K), delete the degree symbol and add 273. When you want to convert kelvins (K) to degrees Celsius (°C), add the degree symbol and subtract 273.

Conversion Ruler:
Fahrenheit, Celcius, Kelvin

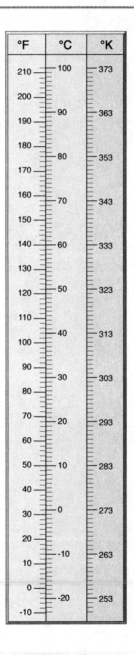